NEW LIVING
SPACES

TIME
LIFE
BOOKS

THE ENCHANTED WORLD
LIBRARY OF NATIONS
HOME REPAIR AND IMPROVEMENT
CLASSICS OF EXPLORATION
PLANET EARTH
PEOPLES OF THE WILD
THE EPIC OF FLIGHT
THE SEAFARERS
WORLD WAR II
THE GOOD COOK
THE TIME-LIFE ENCYCLOPAEDIA OF GARDENING
THE GREAT CITIES
THE OLD WEST
THE WORLD'S WILD PLACES
THE EMERGENCE OF MAN
LIFE LIBRARY OF PHOTOGRAPHY
TIME-LIFE LIBRARY OF ART
GREAT AGES OF MAN
LIFE SCIENCE LIBRARY
LIFE NATURE LIBRARY
THE TIME-LIFE BOOK OF BOATING
TECHNIQUES OF PHOTOGRAPHY
LIFE AT WAR
LIFE GOES TO THE MOVIES
BEST OF LIFE
LIFE IN SPACE

This volume is part of a series offering home
owners detailed instructions on repairs,
construction and improvements which they
can undertake themselves.

HOME REPAIR
AND IMPROVEMENT

NEW LIVING SPACES

BY THE EDITORS OF
TIME-LIFE BOOKS

TIME-LIFE BOOKS
AMSTERDAM

TIME-LIFE BOOKS

EUROPEAN EDITOR: Kit van Tulleken
Assistant European Editor: Gillian Moore
Design Director: Ed Skyner
Photography Director: Pamela Marke
Chief of Research: Vanessa Kramer
Chief Sub-Editor: Ilse Gray

HOME REPAIR AND IMPROVEMENT

EDITORIAL STAFF FOR NEW LIVING SPACES
Editor: Philip W. Payne
Assistant Editor: Edward Brash
Designer: Herbert H. Quarmby
Picture Editor: Adrian G. Allen
Associate Designer: Anne Masters
Staff Writers: Margaret Fogarty, Mary Paul, Ted Sell,
Mark M. Steele
Art Associates: Michelle Clay, Juli Hopfl, Abbe Stein,
Mary B. Wilshire, Richard Whiting
Editorial Assistant: Eleanor G. Kask

EUROPEAN EDITION
Series Director: Jackie Matthews
Editor: Lynn Earnshaw
Writer/Researcher: Margaret Hall
Designers: Paul Reeves (principal), Debbie Martindale
Sub-Editors: Frances Dixon, Hilary Hockman

EDITORIAL PRODUCTION
Chief: Jane Hawker
Production Assistants: Alan Godwin, Maureen Kelly
Picture Co-ordinator: Peggy Tout
Editorial Department: Debra Lelliot, Theresa John

THE CONSULTANTS: Leslie Stokes was a self-employed carpenter and joiner
for seven years, specializing in purpose-made joinery and internal
fittings. Since 1976 he has taught in the building department at the
Hammersmith and West London College.

Bill Webb worked as a licensed builder for six years before joining
the staff of the Granville College of Technical and Further
Education, Sydney, where he now teaches cabinet making, shopfitting
and detailed joinery.

Thomas D. Ball, the general consultant for this book, is a partner in a
contracting firm that specializes in home building and renovation.

Richard Ridley, architectural consultant for the book, founded
an architectural firm that has won awards for urban planning
and residential building. He also writes and illustrates how-to
manuals to encourage clients to participate in the design and
construction of new structures.

Contents

New Rooms the Easy Way

There are times when every home owner feels a little like the old woman who lived in a shoe. Parents trip over toddlers in cramped kitchens. Party-givers juggle food, drinks and guests between small living and dining rooms. Budding scientists and musicians compete for territory in shared bedrooms.

What these people need is new living space. Most houses contain a surprising amount of space that can be altered or adapted to suit a variety of family needs. Attics, garages and basements can be converted into living areas. Porches can be enclosed and converted. Finished interior rooms can be more fully utilized—sometimes by removing walls to open up small rooms, sometimes by installing partitions to divide large rooms for different activities.

Methods for creating new living space will vary according to the structure of your home, the materials from which it is built and your local building regulations. Whether your project consists of a simple folding door or an attic conversion, time spent in careful planning will be rewarded by a more straightforward and satisfying job. Most D.I.Y. shops offer a wide range of easy-to-use materials that will simplify even the most complex jobs. Factory-assembled doors and windows come complete and ready for installation. Modern ceilings, floors and walls are now made of materials and fixtures specifically designed for amateurs to work with.

The simplest way to create new space without changing the structure of your home is to install partitions which act as storage or display units as well. Even basic carpentry can be avoided if you use prefabricated or self-assembly units which can be adapted from their original purpose to act as room dividers. Standard, inexpensive shelves and cabinets can become a wall as well as storage units, if set up freestanding to divide a large space. More elaborate, purpose-made room dividers, designed to fit your own concept of living space, are installed using the same techniques as for a simple bookshelf *(pages 8–9)*.

Wide sliding or folding doors become a movable partition if hung across a large room or alcove. With the doors shut, you have two small, private sections, or a concealed working or sleeping area, while opening the door restores the original space when it is needed. All sliding and folding doors are fitted in basically the same way—a ceiling-mounted track to carry the sliding gear, and aligners fitted to the wall or floor *(pages 14–17)*. Accordion doors *(pages 14–15)* are now available to reach from floor to ceiling, and can be used to create a complete, movable wall. They also come in a range of timber finishes to add dramatically as well as practically to your existing decor.

Ready-Made Dividers—Walls That Are Not Walls

In rooms that serve several functions, such as eating, working, socializing and storage, you can usually create more useful living spaces by separating the functions with various kinds of room dividers. Even the way you arrange furniture can establish areas for specific purposes. More definite spaces can be created by using wood or metal frames with transparent plastic, wood or fabric-covered panels that serve essentially as movable screens.

You can easily divide space by using ready-made units intended for other purposes. Tall bookcases meant to go against a wall can be brought out to the middle of a room and made stable. Storage cabinets, including kitchen cupboards, can be anchored to the floor to create separate areas. At greater expense, heavy dividers, purpose built to close off one part of a room, can also function as bars, desks, bookshelves and television, video or stereo cabinets.

If you choose the kind of room dividers that are built from bookshelves or cupboards—they are generally shallower and lighter than purpose-made dividers—make sure they will not move or topple over. Fas-ten two units back to back (thus hiding the unfinished parts) and fix them to the floor with cleats (below, left). If high enough, they can also be anchored to a concrete or plasterboard ceiling for added stability. Units with a painted or plain wood finish can be nailed to the floor cleats. If you sink the nails and fill the indentations, the fix-ing will be almost invisible.

A heavy, purpose-made room divider must be very securely fixed both at the floor and ceiling. To avoid damaging ex-pensive veneer finishes by nailing, the div-ider has to be firmly wedged at the ceiling to hold it in place by friction. Some manu-facturers supply special fixing devices which can be adjusted to fill the gap be-tween the top of the divider and the ceiling. If these are not supplied, fix the divider to both the floor and the ceiling using cleats, and insert wooden offcuts as packing be-tween the top of the divider and the ceiling cleats. To use this method, you must first measure the height of the ceiling, and buy a room divider 30 to 40 mm shorter than this height to allow space to raise the unit into place and insert the packing.

Cleats to secure a room divider to the floor are fastened in the same way as for a storage unit (below, left); if they are care-fully measured to fit snugly inside the base, they will not need to be nailed to the unit. A concrete ceiling provides a secure anchoring surface for cleats at the top of a heavy divider. For a plasterboard ceiling, the cleats must be fixed to the joists. Estab-lish the spacing and direction of the joists (page 10, Step 1). If the divider runs across the joists, screw the cleats through the plasterboard directly into them. First lo-cate the joist nearest the wall end of the divider, mark its position on the cleat, and drill fixing holes every 400 mm from this point along the cleat. If the joists run parallel to the divider, position the unit so that it runs directly beneath a single joist. Alternatively, install supports between the joists for fixing (page 12, centre).

When the unit is securely wedged, cover the gap at the top by fixing a pelmet, made from matching facing board, over the cleats and packing. Scribe the pelmet to the ceiling to cover any irregularities and to give a perfect finish (opposite page, below).

Anchoring Storage Units

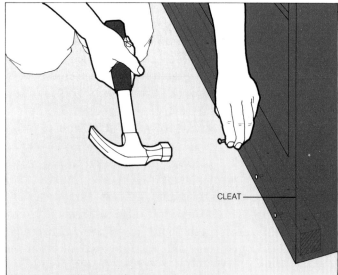

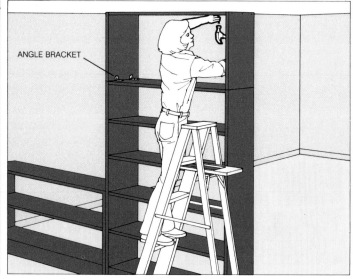

Fastening to the floor. Position the units and out-line their bases. Set the units aside and draw their inside dimensions by measuring in from the outlines a distance equal to the thickness of the unit walls. Cut two pieces of 50 by 50 timber to fit just inside the bottom of the unit. Nail or screw these cleats to the floor. Set the units over the cleats and nail them together (above).

Fastening to the ceiling. Cut two pieces of 25 mm board as wide as the depth of the unit and as high as the distance between the top of the unit and the ceiling. Cut a third piece to nail between them, forming a three-sided box the length of the unit. Finish the wood as desired. Fasten the box to the unit with angle brackets and attach the top of the box to the ceiling (above).

Securing Purpose-Made Dividers

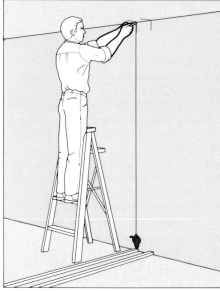

1 **Preparing the cleats.** Cut and fix 50 by 50 mm cleats to the floor *(opposite, left)*. Using a plumb line, mark points on the ceiling directly above each end of the cleats *(above)*; snap chalk lines between them. Cut two 50 by 25 mm ceiling cleats to span the upper face of the unit, and drill holes through them at 400 mm intervals, for 57 mm No. 10 screws if fixing to concrete, or for 50 mm No. 8 screws if fixing to joists.

2 **Fastening the cleats to the ceiling.** Get a helper to hold the first cleat flat along one of the chalk lines, and use a plumb line to check that it runs directly above the corresponding floor cleat. Push a nail through each of the pre-drilled holes to mark the ceiling. Remove the cleat and drill holes in the concrete ceiling or joists to take the fixings you will be using *(Step 1, left)*. For a concrete ceiling, plug the holes and screw the cleat in place. For wooden joists, fix directly to the timber. Repeat the process with the second cleat, which should run along the other chalk line.

With a helper, tilt the room divider so that one edge is raised off the floor, manoeuvre it into position over the floor cleats, then carefully allow it to drop into place.

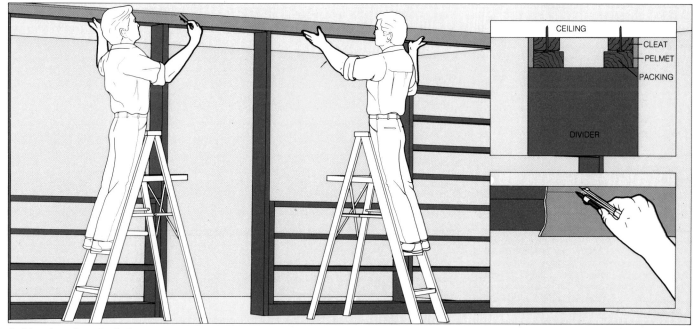

3 **Scribing the pelmet.** Pack the space between the top of the divider and the cleats on each side with wooden offcuts; space the offcuts at regular intervals and ensure that they are flush with the outer edges of the cleats *(top inset)*. Measure the gap between the ceiling and the upper face of the divider at its widest point. Cut two strips of 19 mm facing board the length of the divider and 10 mm wider than the widest gap. Place the first strip against the top of the outer face of the divider, with its upper edge butting the ceiling, and get a helper to hold it in position. Set the legs of a pair of compasses 10 mm apart. Place the point of the compasses on the ceiling and the pencil on the outer face of the facing strip, then run the compasses across the ceiling making sure that the pencil leaves a clear trail *(bottom inset)*. Remove the strip and saw along the scribed line. Repeat the process with the second strip against the other side of the divider. Glue each pelmet to the cleat and packing, using PVA adhesive.

Versatile Partitions Made from Movable Doors

Folding or sliding doors that are hung from or guided by overhead tracks can enclose storage areas or serve as retractable walls that increase the utility of living space. These versatile barriers come in a large variety of shapes, sizes and materials but can be classified generally as accordion, bifold or sliding bypass doors. The accordion and bifold types make handier room dividers than the more cumbersome sliding bypass doors, which are generally used as cupboard doors, but all types can be adapted to serve as room partitions.

Accordion doors are made of pleated fabric or vinyl stretched over a light metal or plastic skeleton. Closing the door stretches out the pleats into a substantial-looking partition; when the door is opened, the pleats fold compactly to one side. They are also available as glazed, moulded or plain wood panels in a variety of different timbers and finishes. Accordion doors, which are hung on rollers from a single overhead track and attached at one side to a wall, are the easiest of the three types of track-mounted doors to install and once in place require little or no adjustment.

Bifold doors consist of wood, plastic or metal panels up to about 600 mm wide, hinged together lengthwise, usually in pairs. Pairs of panels can be linked together to form one continuous surface. Bi-

fold doors consisting of mirror panels are especially effective in creating an illusion of extra space. A bifold door consisting of one or more pairs can be mounted at one side of an opening and closed by pulling it all the way across; or the doors can be installed at each side of an opening and pulled together at the middle. An overhead track guides the bifold door but the weight of the door rests on a pivot that is attached to the floor at the wall side. A pivot at the top of the door holds the assembly upright.

Sliding bypass doors usually consist of two large wood panels, each hung by wheels from its own overhead track. The panels overlap by approximately 30 mm and when they are closed are kept vertically aligned by a small floor-mounted guide. Some models have snap-on or ready-made pelmets to hide exposed sliding gear, or you can easily make one yourself using simple carpentry techniques.

All overhead tracks—whether they support or merely guide a door—sustain considerable stress when the doors are in use and should be attached to a level, structurally supported surface. Accordion doors can often be bought to fit the exact size of your opening, and can therefore be fixed directly to the ceiling joists. For very heavy doors, a header beam should be attached to the joists to support the extra weight. Bifold or

sliding doors are usually made to the height of a normal door: if you are intending to use them as room dividers, you will need to construct a header frame to be suspended from the joists.

The location of the joists helps to determine the position of the door. After locating the joists and marking the proposed position of the door, carefully calculate the vertical space needed for the door and its track. Design and construct a header that is suitable for the type of ceiling involved to fit the space between track and ceiling.

To calculate the height of a header frame to be suspended from a permanently attached ceiling, measure from floor to ceiling at several points along the proposed line of the door. Subtract from the shortest of these measurements (thus allowing for any unevenness in the floor or ceiling) the height of the door and its track, plus the thickness of plasterboard or other covering to be applied to the header. The result is the height of the header frame; its length is, of course, the distance from wall to wall. Attach the header to the ceiling joists, fasten the track to the header and finally mount the door in its track.

For a door that is hung directly from the ceiling, locate the joists and attach the track directly to them through the plasterboard or other ceiling material.

Positioning the Door

1 **Locating the joists.** To locate joists concealed by a permanently attached ceiling, drill a small hole through the ceiling and probe through the hole with a stiff wire to determine the location of the nearest joist and the direction in which it runs. Since joists are usually placed parallel to each other across the narrow dimension of a house, with their centres 400 mm apart, the location of one joist discloses the locations of others. The header for a door mounted parallel to the run of the joists will be attached all along its length to a single joist. To determine the exact location of this joist you may have to probe at two widely separated points. For a header that runs parallel to, but between, two joists, construct the same type of subceiling as for an interior partition in the same position *(page 37, Step 3)*.

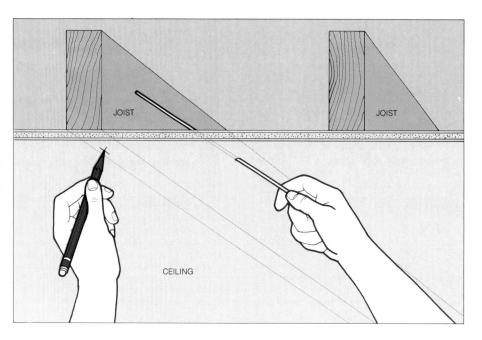

2 Marking the position of the door. Use a chalk line to mark the location of the header. Unreel the chalk-covered line from its housing, hold or fasten it taut across the ceiling from wall to wall along the line to be marked and snap it like a bowstring, leaving a straight, sharp chalk mark across the ceiling. If this line runs at right angles to the joists, mark the position of each joist. These marks, placed a little to one side of the chalk mark, will guide you later when you are attaching the header. Make a vertical chalk mark down the wall at each end of the chalk mark across the ceiling. To make sure the line is vertical, hang a plumb bob at the end of the chalk line, then secure and snap the line. These vertical lines will guide you later in attaching a header frame and attaching and aligning doors.

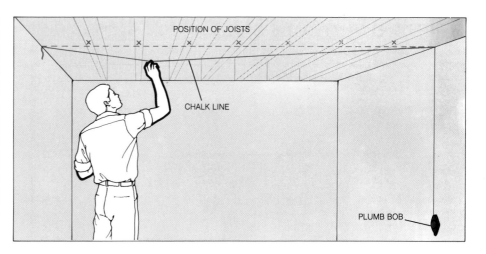

POSITION OF JOISTS

CHALK LINE

PLUMB BOB

Hanging a Header

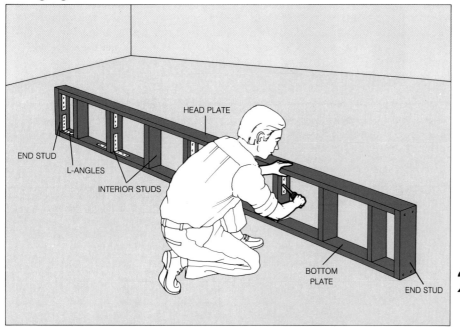

END STUD

L-ANGLES

INTERIOR STUDS

HEAD PLATE

BOTTOM PLATE

END STUD

1 Constructing the header. Build a frame like the one for a non-loadbearing partition wall (*pages 36–37*) using 100 by 50s and 100 mm round-wire nails. Cut the two end vertical studs to the **exact** height of the frame and butt-nail the head **and** bottom plates between them to form a rectangular box. Fill in the box with interior vertical studs nailed 400 mm apart. If the header is to be mounted perpendicular, rather than parallel, to the run of the joists, the first of these interior studs should be nailed 200 mm from one of the end studs, and 400 mm apart thereafter, so that they will not fall directly beneath joists.

Reinforce the frame by attaching metal L-angles inside the angles at each corner, and at the top and bottom of alternate interior studs.

2 Attaching and levelling the header. While a helper holds the frame in place, using the wall and ceiling chalk marks as guides, fasten the sides of the frame to the wall with nails driven part way in. Check the frame with a spirit level.

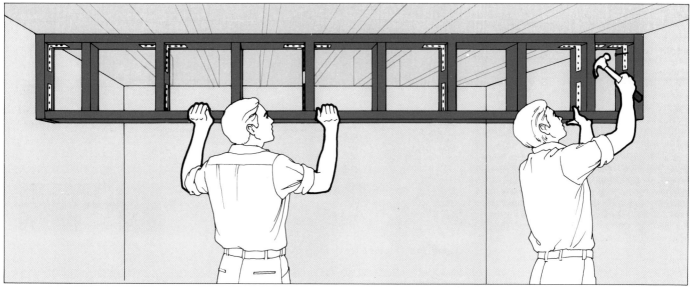

3 **Shimming the frame.** If necessary, level the frame by shimming, that is by driving thin wooden wedges between the head plate and the ceiling. A good shimming technique is to drive in wedges from opposite sides of the head plate to form a tight rectangular block.

4 **Securing the frame.** Once the frame is level, tack it to the joists, then screw it to each joist, or every 600 mm if it is fixed to a single joist, using 6 mm coach screws. Trim off the wedges flush with the frame, if necessary. Finish the frame with plasterboard *(page 42)*.

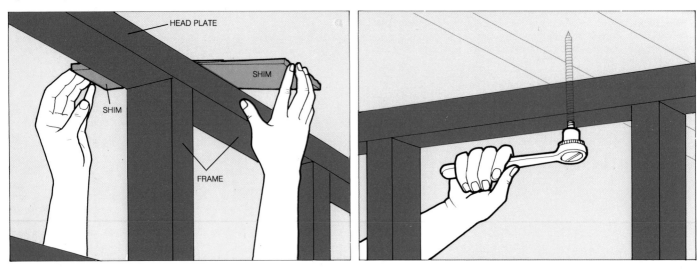

A Header for a Suspended Ceiling: Between Joists

1 **Installing the supports.** To make supports for a header that runs parallel to the joists above a suspended ceiling, cut lengths from 100 by 50 mm timber to fit between two adjoining joists. The header can be suspended from these supports with lengths of a continuously threaded metal rod. With a wood bit 1 mm or so larger than the diameter of the rod, drill a hole through the broad side of each support at its centre. Nail the supports between the two joists at intervals of about 600 mm; the broad sides of the supports should be flush with the bottom edges of the joists.

2 **Attaching the header.** Cut segments of rod to extend from the tops of the supports to the level of the ceiling plus about 75 mm. Insert a length of rod through each support, sandwiching it with two nuts, a washer under the top nut; allow the rods to protrude about 50 mm below the ceiling.

Cut a 100 by 50 the length of the proposed track. Hold it in position, broad side up, and mark the location of each rod. Using an electric drill, make countersink holes at these points with a spade bit the size of the washers you will use. Then drill holes through the header the same size as those in the supports. Attach the header, its countersunk holes down, to the rods, sandwiching it between two nuts on each rod, a washer above the bottom nut. Adjust the nuts on each rod until the top of the header is flush with the ceiling and so that no part of the rod protrudes from the bottom of the header *(inset)*.

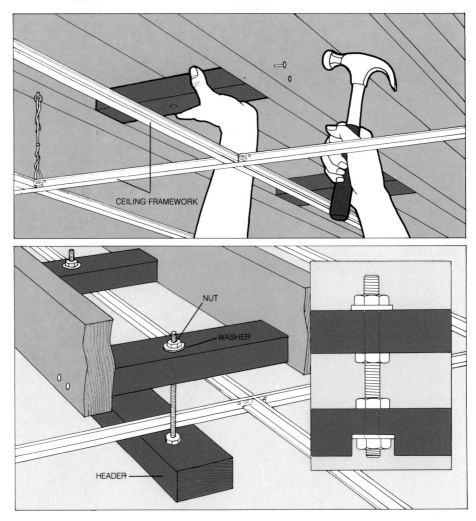

A Header for a Suspended Ceiling: Across Joists

1 **Preparing the support and header.** Cut two 100 by 50s the length of the opening. Remove the cross Ts from the ceiling frame along the line proposed for the door. Hold one of the 100 by 50s up to the joists along this line and mark points on it, about every 600 mm, at which you can insert threaded rods through this support without encountering joists, pipes, ducts or the framework of the ceiling. Drill holes for rods through both of the 100 by 50s, as in Step 2, opposite.

2 **Installing the support and the header.** Attach the support to the bottom edges of the joists along the proposed line of the door. For a heavy door, also attach the support to every other joist with 6 mm coach screws. Connect the header to the support with lengths of rod and level the header, as in Step 2, opposite.

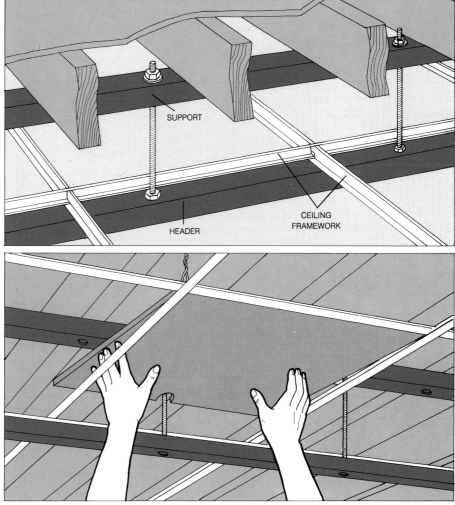

3 **Trimming and replacing ceiling panels.** Align each panel in turn with its space in the grid. Mark on each panel the position of the protruding rod. If the header runs alongside a grid member *(right)*, notch each panel to accommodate the rod and replace the panel. If the header runs between two grid members, cut the panels in half where the header divides them. Notch each of the panels to accommodate the rods and replace them with the notches above the header.

Installing an Accordion Door

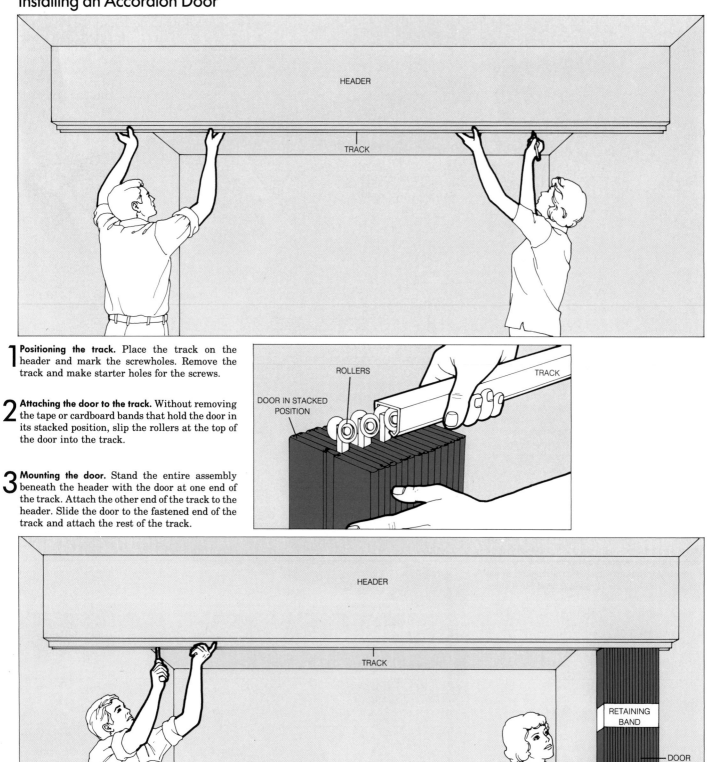

1 **Positioning the track.** Place the track on the header and mark the screwholes. Remove the track and make starter holes for the screws.

2 **Attaching the door to the track.** Without removing the tape or cardboard bands that hold the door in its stacked position, slip the rollers at the top of the door into the track.

3 **Mounting the door.** Stand the entire assembly beneath the header with the door at one end of the track. Attach the other end of the track to the header. Slide the door to the fastened end of the track and attach the rest of the track.

HEADER

TRACK

ROLLERS

TRACK

DOOR IN STACKED POSITION

HEADER

TRACK

RETAINING BAND

DOOR

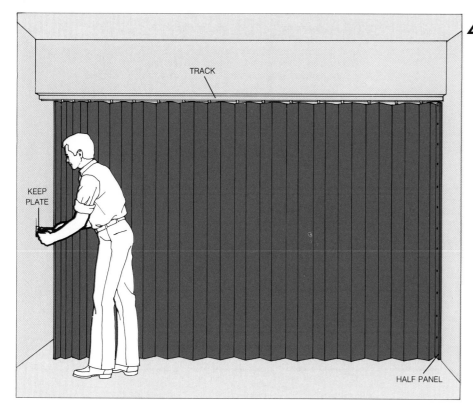

TRACK

KEEP PLATE

HALF PANEL

4 **Positioning the keep plate.** Drop a plumb line from the centre of the track along the wall to which you will attach one side of the door. Along this vertical line, attach the door's wall panel, which is usually a hinged half panel with holes pre-drilled for mounting. Extend the door to the opposite wall. Position the keep plate into which the door latch will fit. Align the keep plate horizontally with the latch and vertically with the centre of the track and attach it to the wall.

Installing Bifold Doors

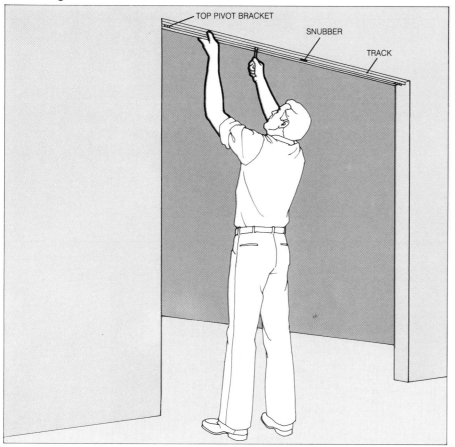

TOP PIVOT BRACKET

SNUBBER

TRACK

1 **Mounting track and top brackets.** Before attaching the track of a bifold door to the header, insert into the track the bracket that holds the pivot for the top of the door and the rubber or plastic snubber that cushions the impact of the door as it closes. When mounting doors on each side of an opening, insert a top pivot bracket at each end of the track with a snubber between them. Then attach the track.

2 **Mounting the bottom pivot bracket.** Slide the top pivot bracket against the wall. Drop a plumb line from the centre of the bracket to the floor. Position the bottom pivot bracket directly beneath the top bracket. Screw the bottom bracket to the wall and to the floor. To provide clearance between the bottom of the door and a carpet, mount the bracket on a small wooden block *(inset)* the thickness of the carpet.

3 **Mounting and positioning the door.** With the door panels folded together, slip the door's bottom pivot into the bottom pivot socket *(bottom inset)*. Slide the top pivot bracket towards the centre of the track and position the door under it. Slip the top pivot socket over the top pivot *(top inset)*. As you push the top pivot bracket and the door back towards the wall, slip the spring-mounted slide guide at the top of the door into the track.

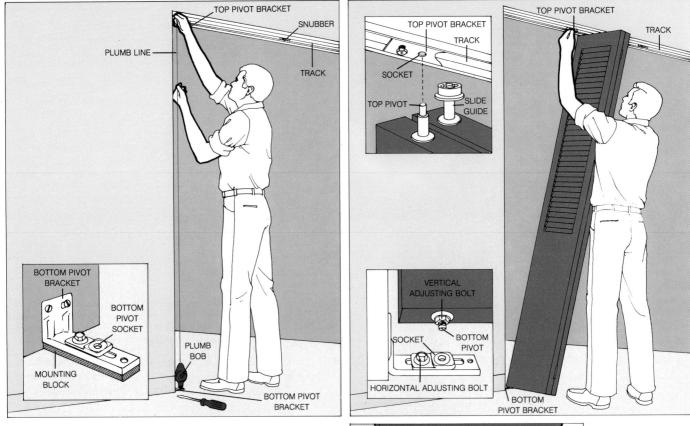

4 **Adjusting the door.** Most manufacturers supply with each door a spanner made to fit the bolts that lock the bottom and top pivot sockets in place. Loosen these bolts, adjust the pivot sockets horizontally until the door extends and folds properly, then tighten the bolts. The door may be raised or lowered slightly by turning the vertical adjusting bolt on the door's bottom pivot *(right)*.

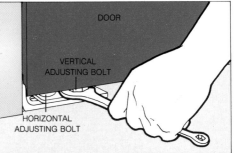

5 **Mounting the aligners.** Bifold doors that are mounted on each side of an opening and meet in the middle when closed are usually held flush and in line with metal aligners. Close the doors and mount one aligner on the back of each door.

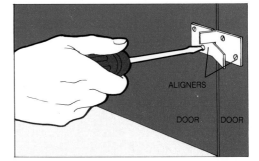

Installing Sliding Doors

1 Hanging the doors. The track for a pair of top-hung sliding bypass doors has two parallel channels. Each door is hung from carriers whose wheels fit into these channels. Proper operation of the doors demands a level header on which to mount the track and careful measurements for the doors themselves. Order sliding doors the height of the opening less 44 mm: 38 mm clearance at the top for the track, and 6 mm at the floor. In width, each door should measure one half of the opening plus 15 mm, to allow a 30 mm overlap when the doors are closed.

Attach the track to the header with the open sides of the two channels towards the rear of the cupboard or other area that the doors will enclose. Hang the innermost door first. Face the closed side of the track. Holding the door with the top tilted away from you, hook the carrier wheels into the rear channel. Hang the other door from the front channel in the same way.

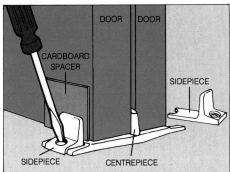

2 Fixing the floor guide. A small two-channelled plastic or metal device which is fastened to the floor at the centre of the opening helps to keep the doors aligned and prevents them from swaying laterally as they slide. A common type of guide is the adjustable three-piece design shown above. To fasten it, hold the doors plumb, insert the centre portion of the floor guide between the doors and attach it to the floor. With the doors hanging free, use a piece of cardboard as a spacer to position each of the two sidepieces about 1 mm from the outside of each door. Fasten the sidepieces to the floor.

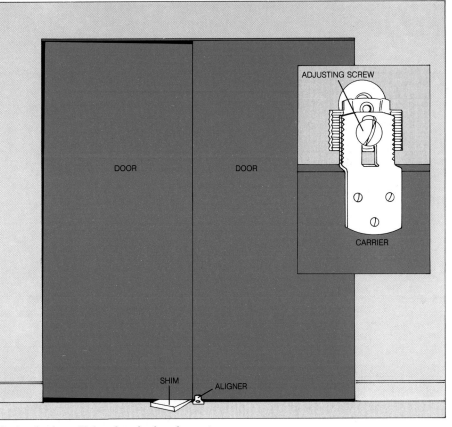

3 Aligning the doors. If the edge of a door does not meet the wall squarely, loosen the adjusting screws on the carriers, push shims between the bottom of the door and the floor until the door squares with the wall, then tighten the screws.

2 Platforms that Remake a Room

A lofty bedroom. A sleeping balcony like the one on the left, photographed just before completion, can make a room of even modest proportions do double duty. The balcony, an elevated platform with a protective rail, provides just enough floor space for a bed and just enough headroom to permit sitting up; the limited space beneath becomes storage or a study. The ship's ladder will be secured to the platform with the framing connectors which are lying on the top step.

When the ancient Greeks devised the amphitheatre of terraced seats surrounding a raised stage, they introduced a design concept that architects have been exploiting ever since: the use of changes in floor and seating levels to create a dramatic effect. A dining area elevated above the floor of the room on a low platform *(pages 20–25)* becomes a special place for meals. Carpeted and cushioned, and stacked in layers, multiple platforms can give a room character as well as built-in comfort. A balcony-like platform on pillars—the gallery—makes an appealing sanctum that paradoxically is partially private and partially on view, and provides both extra storage and new living space *(pages 26–33)*.

Each one of these applications of raised floor sections serves a practical function beyond drama, and practical platforms can be spectacular when several are combined in a large room. They divide living space into areas for specific purposes—eating, conversing, sleeping, working.

Although galleries, balconies and step-up dining areas look different, they all share the same simple structure—a timber frame with a plywood or chipboard floor—and are assembled using straightforward carpentry techniques. Yet they result in such substantial modifications in the design and traffic patterns of the house that they must be well planned. In addition to allowing for the movement of people and the location of doors and windows, you may also need to modify heating, lighting and other electrical installations before beginning construction. A raised platform often blocks heating outlets or radiators. A section of plasterboard will have to be removed so that wall ducts can be extended up to the level of the rim. Similarly, electrical extensions for heaters or cooling fans—either pipes or wires—must be installed before the platform is assembled so that the heating units can be remounted at points along the walls where they will be the most effective.

Before you begin construction, consider how you intend to carry the large framing members into the room, where you will stack them, and how you will move them into place without damaging the room. Remember that a substantial stock of boards will be needed, and it is easy to pack the room with so many building materials that there is barely space to wield a hammer. But it is also important to plan to collect your materials in the room in which the platform is to be assembled, and to leave them to acclimatize to the humidity level of the room for at least two weeks before starting work. This will prevent any further warping or distortion of the timbers after they have been installed.

A Raised Floor to Create Space and Character

Platforms that are built with the solidity and permanence of the floor below them offer interesting and attractive alternatives to walls and furniture as a way of reorganizing living space.

Imaginative use of a raised floor can re-shape a large room to focus on specific areas, or it can separate functional areas in a small room. A low platform, for example, can be used to create a dining area without dividing a room, or it can become a pedestal for a bed, defining the sleeping area and adding character to the bedroom. In multiple levels, and softened with carpets and cushions, platforms can take the place of couches or chairs, creating an impression of comfort and informality.

Like any large permanent structure, a platform must be carefully planned. Begin by measuring the ceiling height. Although stacked platforms can rise to any height, you should aim to have at least 2 metres between the highest platform and the ceiling, to allow adequate headroom.

From this point on, most of your planning can be done on a sketch, on which you should mark the position of existing doors, windows, radiators and electric points. Add the outline of the platform, and consider its effect on traffic patterns through the room. Adjust your platform design, or plan to relocate fixtures if necessary.

Now locate each joist that runs below the platform *(page 10, Step 1)* and mark them on your plan. This is important because the new joists that support the platform floor must either lie directly over the existing floor joists or be at right angles to them. On your drawing, specify exact dimensions for the front and back of the platform frame parallel to—but not necessarily over—the floor joists. Add sides, and then dividers parallel to the sides and no more than 2700 mm apart; if the platform runs two-thirds the length of the floor joists, use at least two dividers. Finally, indicate the positions of 100 by 50 mm platform joists running between the sides and dividers and exactly over or at right angles to the floor joists. If your floor surface is very uneven, the front and sides of the platform should be scribed to fit *(page 9, Step 3)* before the platform is assembled.

Cut and assemble the frame from planed 25 mm general structural grade timber *(Steps 1 and 2)*, drilling holes in the sides, front and dividers to allow for ventilation and to prevent moisture from damaging the wood. When it is fixed to the wall *(Step 3)*, the platform is supported by anchors made from 100 by 50 mm blocks secured to the floor, and it is covered by plywood or chipboard floor panels which are nailed to the frame and joists.

To create a multi-level platform, combine simple rectangular platforms to make the shape you want. The top of a lower platform can double as a step up to a higher one, or you can stack boxes side by side as separate steps. Building regulations state that a step should be no more than 220 mm high, and its tread, or depth, should not be less than 220 mm.

The top of a lower platform can double as a seat, the frame of a platform above serving as a back rest. A seat that will be carpeted should be 350 to 400 mm high and 600 to 650 mm deep; a back 350 to 400 mm high is standard. Cushioned seats can be 200 to 300 mm off the floor—the cushions bring the height up to 400 mm. Set the back of a cushioned seat 760 to 800 mm from the front. The front edge of a platform seat should overhang the frame by 100 mm to provide heel space.

On your room plan, add the outline of an upper level platform, aligning its dividers and joists with those of the lower platform. If the side of an upper platform does not rest on the side of the lower one, add an extra divider to the lower platform in this position. If the front or back of an upper platform does not align with the lower one, add extra joists to the lower one.

If you do not plan to carpet the platform, consider fitting tongue and groove floorboards instead of chipboard panels; the boards and frame can be stained and varnished to give an elegant finish.

Building a Platform

1 Assembling the frame. Arrange the parts of the frame—front, back, sides and dividers—on the floor near the frame's final location. Drill 25 mm ventilation holes along the bottom edges of the front, sides and dividers. Attach the sides and dividers to the front and back of the frame, using 50 mm No. 8 screws: position the screws 25 mm from the top and bottom of the frame *(right)*.

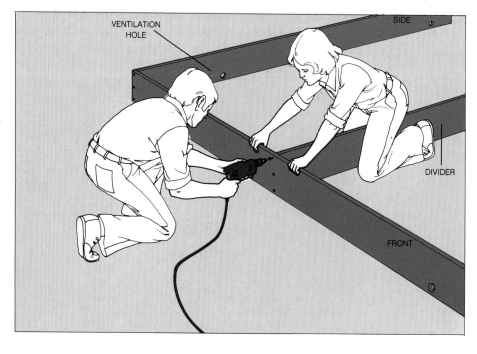

2 **Installing the joists.** Face-nail 100 by 50 mm joists between the sides and dividers, flush with the top of the frame and spaced to be directly over or at right angles to the joists below the floor of the room when the platform is in its final position. Where platform joists meet on each side of a divider, butt-nail one joist and drive the nails at an angle through the divider and into the end of the other joist *(inset)*, using 75 mm round-head or lost-head nails.

As you install the joists, and again after you have moved the frame into position, check the frame for squareness by measuring diagonally across the top in both directions; if necessary, shift the frame by pushing or hammering it until the measurements are equal. Check the frame on all four sides using a spirit level, and insert shims under the frame to level the entire assembly.

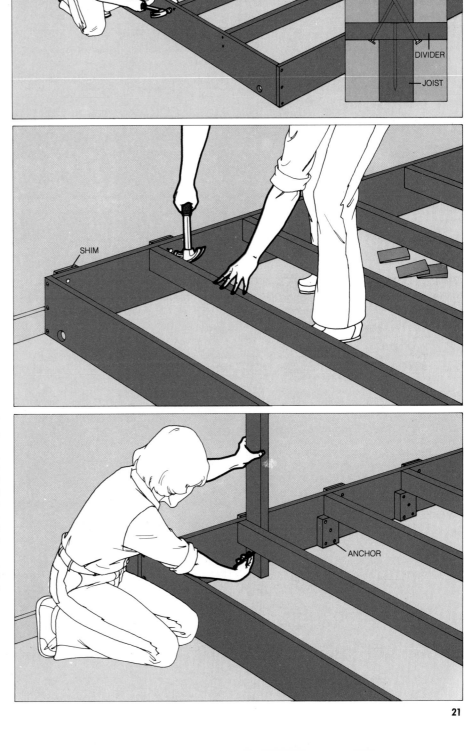

3 **Fastening the frame to a wall.** If you are attaching the platform to a timber frame wall, fix the frame at each stud; if attaching to a masonry wall, space fixings every 300 to 400 mm. Fill the gap between the frame and the wall at each fixing point with wooden shims, and tack the frame and the shims together *(right)*. Secure the frame to the wall, using 6 mm coach screws for timber studs, and 63 or 75 mm No. 10 screws and plugs for masonry, drilling through the frame and shims into the wall.

At each gap between the wall and the corner of the frame above the skirting board, snugly fit a filler strip made of layers of plywood 50 mm wide, and drive nails through the frame and filler strip into the wall.

4 **Anchoring the platform.** Stand a length of 100 by 50 mm timber beside each end of each platform joist, mark it at the bottom of the joist *(right)*, and cut it at the mark. Set the cut piece, called an anchor, under the end of the joist and nail it to the side or divider, and toenail it to the floor. Fit additional anchors flush with the top of the front and back of the frame where they meet the sides and dividers, and at 400 mm intervals between these points; screw these anchors to the frame with 63 mm No. 8 screws, driven in pairs at 75 mm intervals along the anchor.

Remove the shims under the frame and, if you do not plan to carpet the platform, nail a quadrant strip round the base, mitring the corners to give a neat finish *(pages 52–53)*.

5 **Fitting the platform floor.** Lay a plywood or chipboard panel across the joists and use a steel square to align its edges parallel to the frame *(right)*. If the platform fits into a corner, start fitting the floor from that point; if there is any gap of more than 12 mm between the edge of the floor panel and the wall, scribe the sheet to fit. At the last joist completely covered by the panel, trim the edge of the panel to cover 18 mm of the joist. Where a panel edge crosses joists, centre 100 by 50 mm struts between the joists to support the edge when the floor is installed.

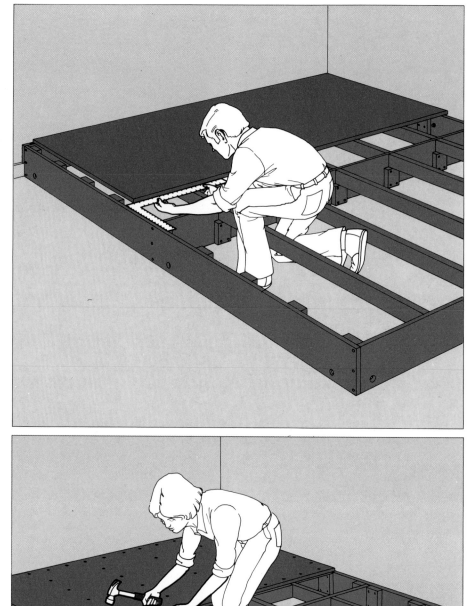

6 **Securing the floor.** Nail or screw the panel to the frame and joists at 200 to 250 mm intervals, and at the centre of each strut, using 60 mm lost-head nails or 37 mm No. 8 chipboard screws. Secure the other sections of the floor, with a 3 mm gap between panels. Trim panels that overhang the platform flush with the frame.

Carpeting a Raised Platform for Comfort

A layer of carpet makes a platform complete. The carpet and its underlay cover the rough edges, muffle footsteps and make an inviting surface on which to sit or recline.

Almost any jute-backed carpet can be used if installed over underlay, though shag styles are a poor choice for a platform with steps—the sparse pile wears badly. The best underlay for a platform is a wool-hair mix felt or canvas-backed rubber.

You will need about 2 per cent more underlay than the area of the platform top and sides. Buy enough carpet to cover the platform completely, allowing 75 mm extra in each direction for trimming. The pile direction will determine the alignment of the carpet along the platform: the pile should run down the main edge—the edge most often used to step on to the platform.

The carpet is held to the floor by stretching it over a carpet gripper—a plywood strip with projecting pinpoints which hook into the carpet—which is nailed round the perimeter of the platform, pinpoints out and pointing downwards. You will also need a knee-kicker—a specialized tool which is available at hire shops, that hooks an end of the carpet so that you can stretch

the carpet to a strip by repeatedly kicking the tool with your knee.

If the platform is too large to be covered by a single width of carpet, you must plan to seam pieces together with 50 to 75 mm-wide hessian tape and white fabric glue after the carpet has been stretched into place. Position the carpet so that the two edges butt against each other, making sure that the pile runs in the same direction on both sides of the join. Open up the seam and lay the tape, hessian side up, on the platform floor, along the length of the seam. Pour a 25 mm-wide bead of glue down the centre of the tape, then, using the pile side of a small offcut of carpet, spread the glue evenly across the width of the tape. Use the offcut to coat the underside of each carpet edge with glue up to half the width of the tape. Hold the carpet away from the tape for about five minutes, then press the two together and walk up and down the seam to ensure good adhesion.

The platform shown here, like the example opposite, is enclosed by walls on two adjacent sides, but you can carpet any platform by following the same procedures. Stretch the carpet along two sides first,

leaving about 150 mm at each end unfastened. To stretch the remaining sides, start each at the end of one of the first two.

To carpet a seat which overhangs the frame, fasten the carpet with tacks at the front of the seat, fold it under the overhang and fasten it there with tacks or carpet adhesive. Use a separate strip of carpet for the platform sides underneath the seat.

Whatever the configuration of your platform, prepare it for carpeting in the same way. On the free sides, round the vertical and the top-to-side corners with a rasp or a router. Then, before installing carpet gripper, sweep the platform and room.

If you are covering the platform with foam-backed carpet, make sure that it is a hard-wearing variety, and do not use underlay. Lay the carpet in the same order as for a jute-backed carpet, stapling or nailing the carpet at the edges instead of stretching it over carpet gripper. To fit the corners, make the same cuts and folds as described on page 25, Step 5, but, before folding, scrape off enough foam backing to make the folded section the same thickness as an open piece of carpet, then tack the folded edges into place.

Laying the Carpet

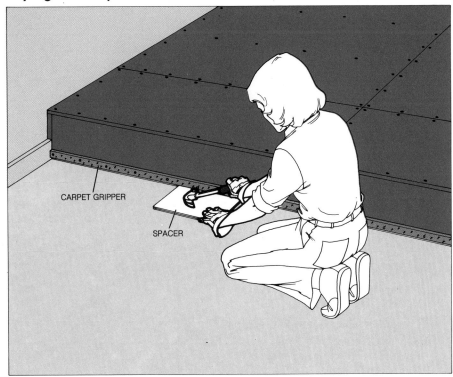

CARPET GRIPPER

SPACER

1 **Installing carpet gripper.** Wearing gloves, nail carpet gripper along the bottom of the platform and along the top next to the walls. Position the strip with its angled pins pointing away and down from the area to be carpeted, and with a 5 mm gap between the strips and the wall or floor. To set the gap, use a spacer made of layers of cardboard glued together; push the strip to keep the gap constant along an uneven floor or wall. Cut the strip 35 mm short of each outside corner and, on a platform with a step, 35 mm short of outside corners formed by the intersection of the platform and the step.

On a step, install the carpet gripper as you would on a platform, but set the gripper at the back of the tread and the side of the platform to leave a gap of 10 mm between them, with the pins of the strips pointing towards each other. To carpet a room and platform at the same time, join the room and platform carpet as you would the sections of carpet on a stair tread and platform side *(page 25, below)*.

2 **Laying underlay.** Within the area bounded by the carpet gripper, lay widths of underlay, fabric side up, to overlap the gripper; staple the edges of each piece to the platform at 150 mm intervals, and use a trimming knife held at a 45-degree angle to trim the underlay to a bevelled edge even with the inner edge of the gripper. Trim underlay flush to the walls and skirting boards beside the platform, then seal underlay seams with cloth tape. At the top of an outside corner, trim each piece of underlay away from the corner at a 45-degree angle to a point 35 mm from the corner, then cut straight down to the floor (inset); at the inside corner of a step, trim the padding back 35 mm.

Arrange the carpet on the platform with its pile pointing down the main edge and with at least 10 mm of overlap along the floor and up the walls. Where each platform side meets the wall, cut the edges of the carpet to make it lie flat.

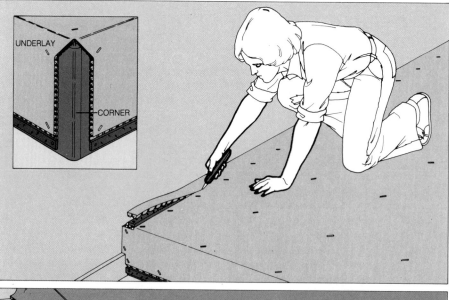

3 **Stretching carpet along the main edge.** At one end of the main platform edge, press the carpet on to the pins of the carpet gripper with the face of a hammer, and spot-nail the carpet to the gripper with a 25 mm round-wire nail driven part way in; then, at the other end of the main edge, push the point of an awl through the carpet and into the carpet gripper. Use the awl to prise the carpet edge sideways along the gripper, stretching it taut, then press the carpet on to the carpet gripper and spot-nail it 150 mm from the end. Working between the spot nails, press the carpet edge on to the carpet gripper, and secure it temporarily with strips of wood tacked over the gripper. Stretch the adjacent edge of the carpet, starting at the corner and working towards the wall.

On a main edge with a step, cut the carpet roughly round the step, then stretch from the wall to the step, along the tread of the step and from the step to the corner, driving in spot nails at the beginning and end of each stretch.

4 **Using the knee-kicker.** Starting at a wall and working on hands and knees, hold a carpet knee-kicker, spikes adjusted to the carpet thickness, with the hand that is closer to the corner of the room. Set the knee-kicker at a 45-degree angle to the wall and, pointing into the corner, position the head of the kicker about 25 mm from the wall. Kick the pad of the tool with the knee that is closer to the corner, to stretch the carpet and hook it on to the carpet gripper. Move along the wall, hooking the carpet as you go and holding it hooked with your free hand. Repeat on the adjacent wall, then trim the carpet to an overlap of 10 mm up the wall. Tuck the overlap into the gap between the wall and the carpet gripper with a blunt bolster or screwdriver blade.

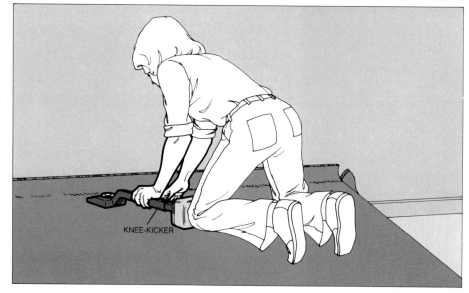

5 **Fitting the carpet to an outside corner.** Starting 25 mm from the platform, slit the carpet diagonally away from the corner; then continue the slit back upwards, from the starting point, to the rounded top of the corner, and fold the triangular waste pieces back. Trim these flaps so that 30 mm will project beyond the corner, and trim 75 mm from the bottom of each flap so that it is flush with the floor. Turn the flaps under to achieve the best-looking fit, then spot-nail them in place.

6 **Stitching the corner.** Thread a curved carpet needle with waxed carpet thread, make a large knot in the long end and, starting at the back of the carpet, loop the needle through a folded edge of the carpet at the top of the corner. Pull the thread through, loop the needle into the carpet edge opposite this stitch, and guide the needle inside the carpet to bring it out 15 to 20 mm below the entry point; then pull the thread taut. Continue this over-and-down pattern to the bottom of the corner. There, drive a

20 mm round-wire nail part way in and loop the thread round it a few times; then drive the nail all the way in and snip off the thread.

To complete the fitting, trim the carpet flush with the walls and skirting boards beside the platform. Remove the spot nails from the carpet and the wood strips holding the carpet down over the carpet gripper. Trim the carpet along the floor edge of the platform, leaving an overlap of 10 mm; tuck this under the carpet gripper using a blunt bolster or screwdriver blade.

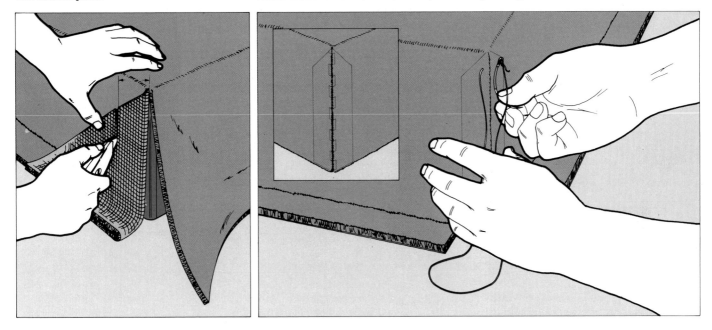

Covering a Step

Stretching the carpet. Lay the carpet with its pile pointing down the step and press it on to a carpet gripper at the bottom of the riser, then use a knee-kicker angled away from the centre of the step to stretch it on to a carpet gripper at the back of the tread. Trim the waste above the step with a trimming knife held on its side on the tread, then tuck the remainder into the space behind the gripper with a blunt bolster.

Use the knee-kicker to stretch the carpet down the sides of the step on to the middle of a carpet gripper at the bottom of each side and spot-nail it. Trim and sew the outside corners (Steps 5 and 6, above); finish the back corners by trimming the carpet, turning it under and tacking the flaps with round-wire nails. Stretch the carpet on to the remainder of the carpet gripper on each side and remove the spot nails.

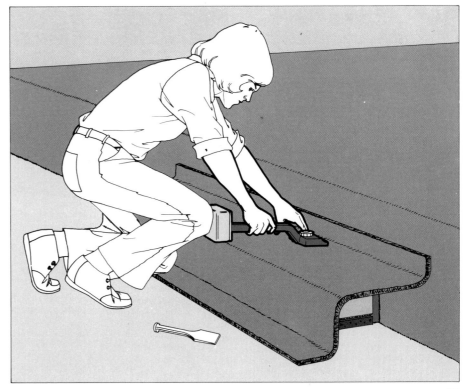

Raised Platforms: Balconies to Stretch a Room

In a room with high ceilings, you can create extra living space by constructing a balcony, either as a sleeping platform or as a gallery which provides an entire room. For a complete second-storey room, you need an existing ceiling at least 4.8 metres high—most building regulations require a minimum headroom of 2.4 metres in any living space. However, a child's sleeping platform with about 1.5 metres above it— enough for a person to sit on the bed—can be built into a room with a ceiling as low as 3.5 metres. Extra space created beneath a platform can be used for storage.

The materials you will use for building a platform are standard: general structural-grade planed timber for the frame and joists, plywood or chipboard panels for flooring, and 19 mm facing boards to cover exposed edges of the frame. The maximum spans for joists spaced at 400 mm intervals are roughly: 150 by 50 mm—2.8 metres; 200 by 50 mm—3.5 metres; 300 by 50 mm—4.5 metres. Building methods are straightforward, but you will need help for some of the work.

Access is by a ladder, with treads supported by wooden cleats, and, for safety, firmly fixed hand and knee rails. A low protective railing round a sleeping platform should be at least 600 to 700 mm high, with railing posts a maximum of 100 mm apart; a railing for a large platform should be a minimum of 1 metre above the deck, and must be sturdy enough to bear an adult's weight. To use the space under a gallery for storage, construct a standard 100 by 50 mm stud partition wall *(pages 36–39)* as a frame for cupboards.

A sleeping platform. This simple balcony is set a minimum of 1.5 metres beneath the ceiling. The outer end is supported by heavy posts which are fixed to the floor with metal brackets, and the inner end is secured to the wall. The frame consists of general structural-grade planed timber, except for decorative facing boards fastened to exposed frame edges; the flooring consists of plywood or chipboard panels. A ladder provides access, and the railing posts are spaced closely enough to protect a small child from danger.

A large-scale gallery. This platform spans the space between two load-bearing walls and has enough headroom for an adult to stand. Its plywood or chipboard floor is supported by full-scale joists, which hang on ledgers bolted to the wall. The staircase ladder has a hand and knee rail for safety. For balconies as big as this one, most building regulations require a strong railing at least 1 metre high.

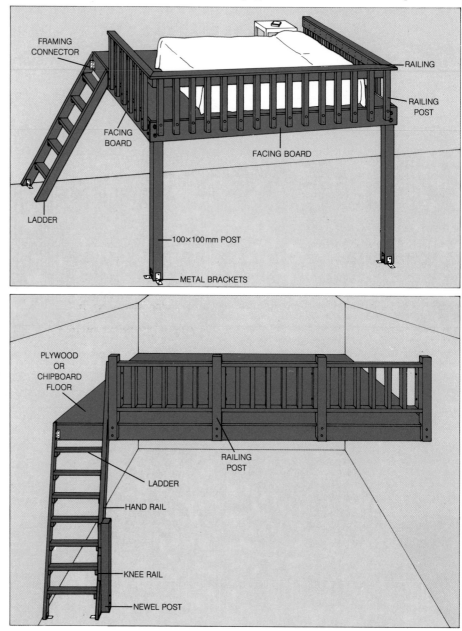

Building a Sleeping Platform

1 Installing the ledger. Using a chalk line and a spirit level, mark the position of the bottom of the platform on the wall. For a masonry wall, make marks below this line at 600 mm intervals to indicate the position of the drill holes. Cut a 100 by 50 mm ledger to the length of the platform, and set it against the wall with its top edge against the marked line and each end about halfway between a pair of drill marks. Nail the ledger temporarily in place *(right)*. Drill holes through the ledger and the wall for 75 or 87 mm No. 10 screws, and fasten the ledger to the wall. For a stud wall, use 9 mm coach screws, 100 mm long, to attach the ledger to each stud.

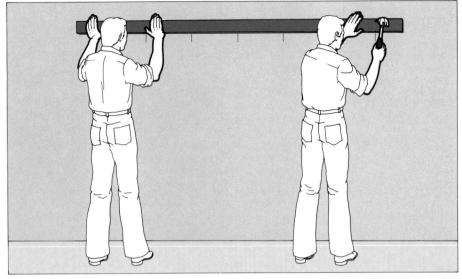

2 Assembling the platform frame. Working on the floor, build a rectangular framework of joists nailed between two header joists—in this example all the joists are 150 by 50 mm. Mark the headers for joist centres 400 mm apart and face-nail each end of a joist in place with three 100 mm round-wire nails; use a combination square to check for right angles.

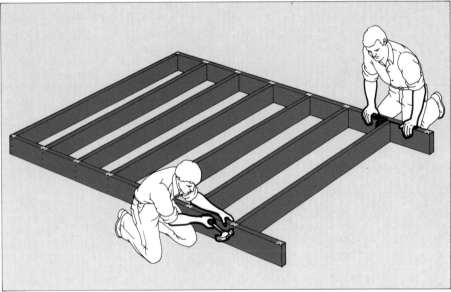

3 Completing the frame. Nail 100 by 50 mm strutting between the joists at the points where the edges of the flooring panels will meet. Attach 19 mm chipboard panels to the frame and struts, using 63 mm lost-head nails *(page 22, Step 6)*.

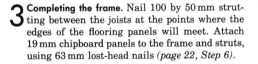

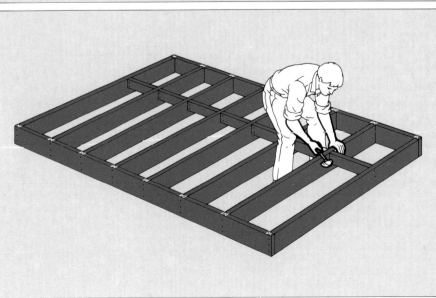

4 **Attaching facing boards.** Cut three 19 mm boards, long enough to fit round the three exposed sides of the platform and wide enough to cover the joist sides and the edges of the floor panels. Turn the platform bottom side up. Nail the boards to the joists, their tops flush with the top of the floor panels, by driving three 50 mm oval or lost-head nails at the ends and additional nails every 400 mm in a staggered pattern.

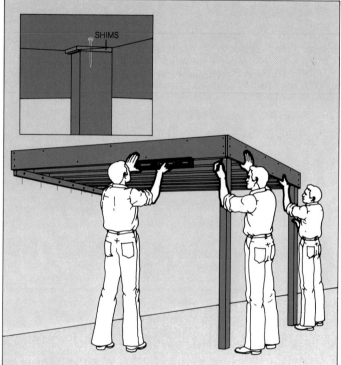

5 **Raising the platform.** Cut two 100 by 100 mm posts to the height of the bottom of the platform floor and, with helpers, lift the platform into place. Rest the rear header joist on the ledger and, while one helper holds this header against the wall, set the 100 by 100 mm posts within the forward corners formed by the front header and the end joists. Above each of the ledger's fixing positions, drill pilot holes through the rear header and into the wall or studs and fasten the header to the wall with screws the same size as those you used on the ledger.

6 **Bolting the posts in place.** While your helpers steady the posts, use a level to check that the platform is level both parallel and perpendicular to the wall, then get the helpers to mark the posts at the bottoms of the joists. If a post is too long, trim it. If one is too short, drive shims between the top of the post and the platform (*inset*). When the wedges hold the platform at the marks on the posts, drive a nail through the floor and wedges into the tops of the posts.

With the post marks aligned with the bottoms of the joists, drill holes through the joists and posts for two 6 mm coach bolts at the front and two at the sides of each corner, staggering the holes so the bolts do not intersect.

7 **Securing the posts to the floor.** Check that the front and sides of each post are plumb, and mark the floor at the bottoms of the posts for reference. Fix each post to the floor using four table stretcher plates or pieces of L-angle cut to the thickness of the post; use 32 mm No. 8 steel screws to attach the plates to each side of the post and the floor *(inset)*.

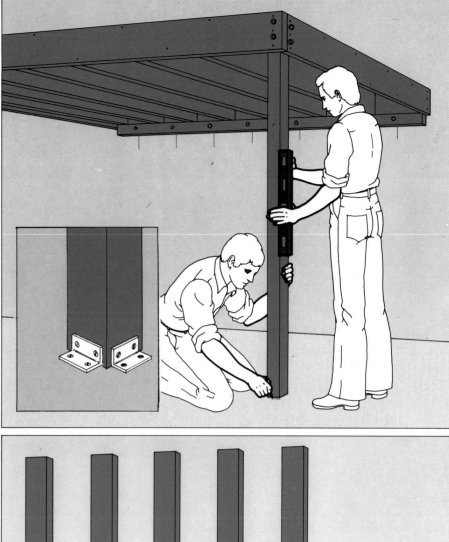

8 **Setting posts for a railing.** Cut railing posts 150 mm longer than the required height from 50 by 50 mm planed timber. Nail each one to the facing board of the platform, overlapping the facing board by 150 mm. Space posts not more than 100 mm apart; leave an opening at least 650 mm wide for the entrance to the platform.

Plumb each post with a level, drill a hole for a 6 mm coach bolt 75 mm below the platform floor, and bolt the railing post in place.

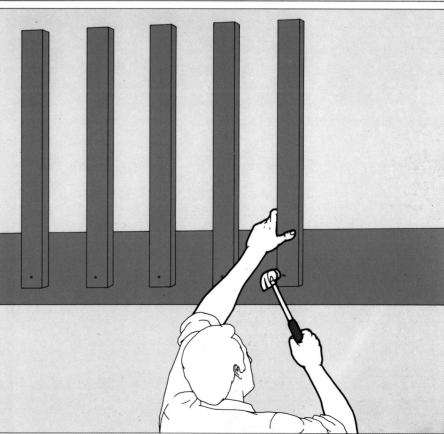

9 **Topping the railing.** Hold a planed 150 by 25 mm board flat along the inside of each row of posts, flush with the post tops, and screw the board in place *(right)*. Attach planed 100 by 25 mm boards—cut at the corners for mitre or butt joints—flat on top of the posts, with one edge flush with the inner faces of the 150 by 25s *(inset)*, and nail these topping boards to the posts and to the 150 by 25s.

Construct and attach a ladder *(pages 32–33)*.

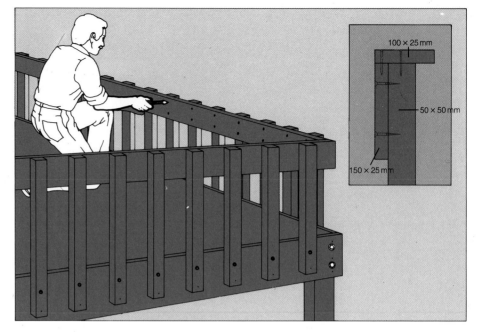

Building a Gallery

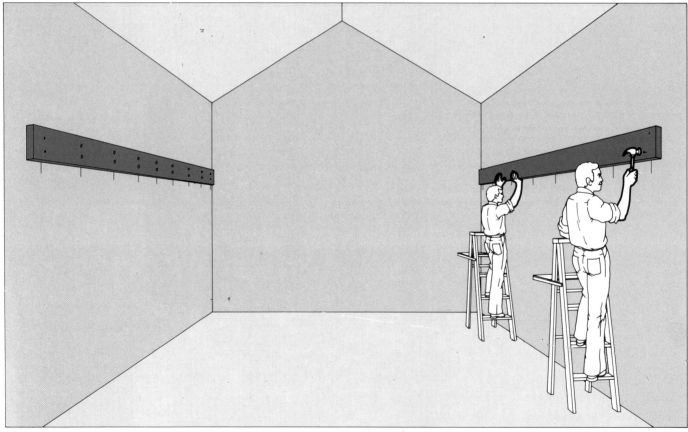

1 **Installing the ledgers.** Mark the positions of the ledgers and fixings on opposite walls *(page 27, Step 1)* and cut the ledgers—in this example 225 by 50 mm—so that each one reaches from a corner to a point 125 mm beyond the outermost fixing point. With the aid of a helper, nail the ends of each ledger to the wall; for a masonry wall, use two 75 or 87 mm masonry nails at each point. For a timber stud wall, nail to a stud near the corner, and to the outermost stud, using 100 mm round-wire nails at each point. Drill two pilot holes through the ledgers and into each intermediate stud for 9 mm coach screws, or into masonry for 75 or 87 mm No. 10 screws at 400 mm intervals, and fasten the ledgers in place.

2 **Installing the joists.** At 400 mm intervals, nail joist hangers to the ledgers, bottoms of the hangers flush with the bottoms of the ledgers. Fit the joists in place—if a joist has a bow, set it upwards—and nail the joists to the hangers.

3 **Laying down the floor.** Cut struts from joist stock and nail them between joists where the edges of the floor panels will meet. Fit panels of 19 mm plywood or chipboard *(page 22)*. If you intend to carpet the platform, extend the flooring panels 35 mm beyond the front joist. When you install a facing board directly below the flooring panels *(Step 4, below)*, the part of the overhang that projects over the board will form a 12 mm lip to shape and secure the edge of the carpet.

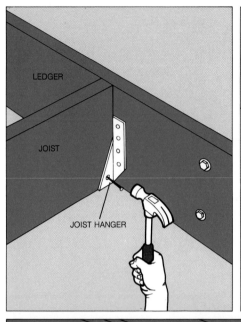

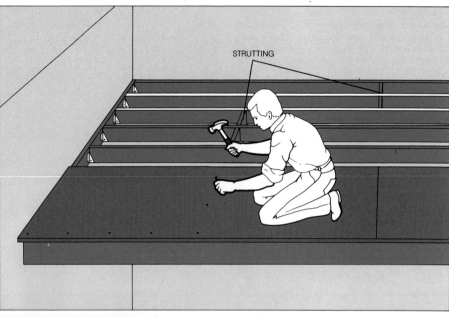

4 **Putting up a plasterboard ceiling.** Make a T-brace of 100 by 50s to the height of the ceiling under the gallery. While a helper supports each plasterboard panel with the brace, nail it in place with 37 mm plasterboard nails. Finish the ceiling with plasterboard tape and jointing compound *(pages 46–47)*. Nail a facing board across the front of the platform, covering the edge of the plasterboard as well. For an uncarpeted gallery, set the top of the facing board flush with the top of the floor panels, exactly as you would for a sleeping platform *(page 28, Step 4)*. If you are planning to carpet the floor of the gallery, as here, set the top of the facing board directly against the underside of the overhanging floor panels.

5 **Building a railing.** Cut 1.4 metre posts from planed 100 by 100s, and make a notch 25 mm deep and 240 mm long at one end of each post. Using coach screws, fix the posts to the gallery frame at 1.2 metre intervals, centre to centre, with the notches against the facing boards; if the gallery floor has an overhang for carpet, notch the floor panels to receive the posts. Build rectangular frames of planed 100 by 50s, each 1100 by 950 mm, and fill the frames with planed 100 by 50 mm balusters spaced at 150 mm intervals, centre to centre. With a helper, set a frame between each pair of posts, with the top of the frame 100 mm below the tops of the posts. Attach each frame side to a post with two coach screws. Leave a space open for the gallery entrance.

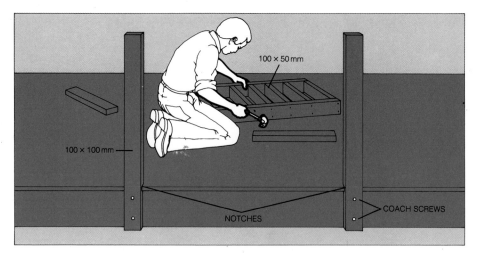

A Staircase Ladder

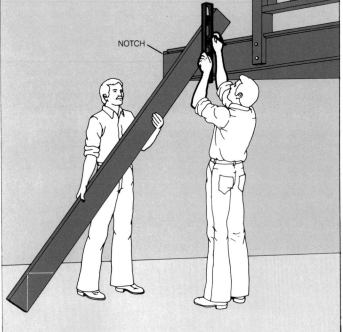

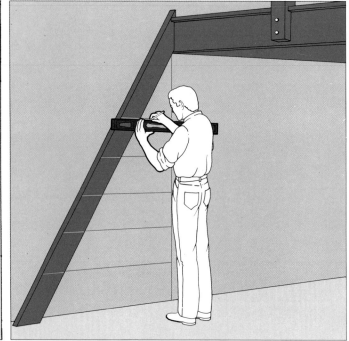

1 **Marking the stringers.** After notching overhanging floor panels, in this example for a 675 mm opening, set a planed 150 by 50 mm stringer against the top of the platform at the angle of the ladder—typically about 60 degrees. Using a level, mark the top of the stringer with a vertical line directly upwards from the edge of the platform (above). Measure the length of the vertical line, and measure the same distance up from the bottom corner of the stringer. At this point, draw a horizontal line across the stringer with a level. Cut the board at both lines and use it as a template to cut a second stringer.

2 **Installing cleats.** The distance between treads should be about 220 mm. To determine the number of treads, divide the height from the floor to the top of the platform by 220 and round up to the nearest whole number. Divide this number into the height to give you the spacing of the treads. Draw a vertical line from the top of the platform to the floor and mark the tread positions on it. To mark the cleat lines, position a stringer against the wall and fix it to the platform; use a level to transfer the tread marks (above). Take the stringer down, and duplicate the lines on the second stringer. For the cleats, cut 140 mm lengths of 50 by 25 mm planed timber; fix them in place on the insides of the stringers, tops flush with the lines, and front top corners flush with the front of the stringers, using PVA glue and four 50 mm No. 8 screws per cleat.

3 **Completing and securing the ladder.** Cut planed 150 by 50 mm treads, here 575 mm wide. Set them on the cleats and secure them with glue and 63 mm lost-head nails driven through the stringers and into the ends of the treads. Raise the ladder into position and secure the stringers at the top with framing connectors, and at the bottom with table stretcher plates or L-angles.

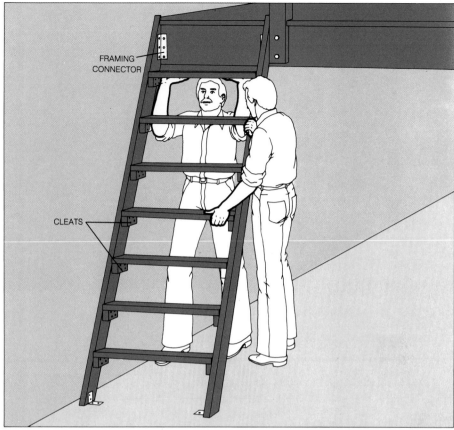

FRAMING CONNECTOR

CLEATS

4 **Attaching hand and knee rails.** Cut a planed 75 by 75 mm newel post to the same height as the platform's railing posts. Position the newel at the foot of the outer stringer, so that it covers the complete width of the stringer. Fix the post to the stringer above and below the first tread, using two 9 mm coach screws fixed into the newel from the inside of the stringer (inset).

Cut two rails the same length as the stringers from 100 or 150 by 32 mm planed timber; if the space between them would be more than 100 mm, install an extra rail. Screw the hand and knee rails to the inside of the newel and the railing post next to the opening. Trim the top and bottom ends of the rails and the bottom of the stringers vertically, to give a neat finish.

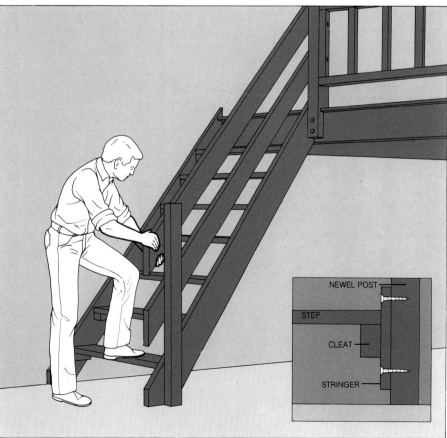

NEWEL POST

STEP

CLEAT

STRINGER

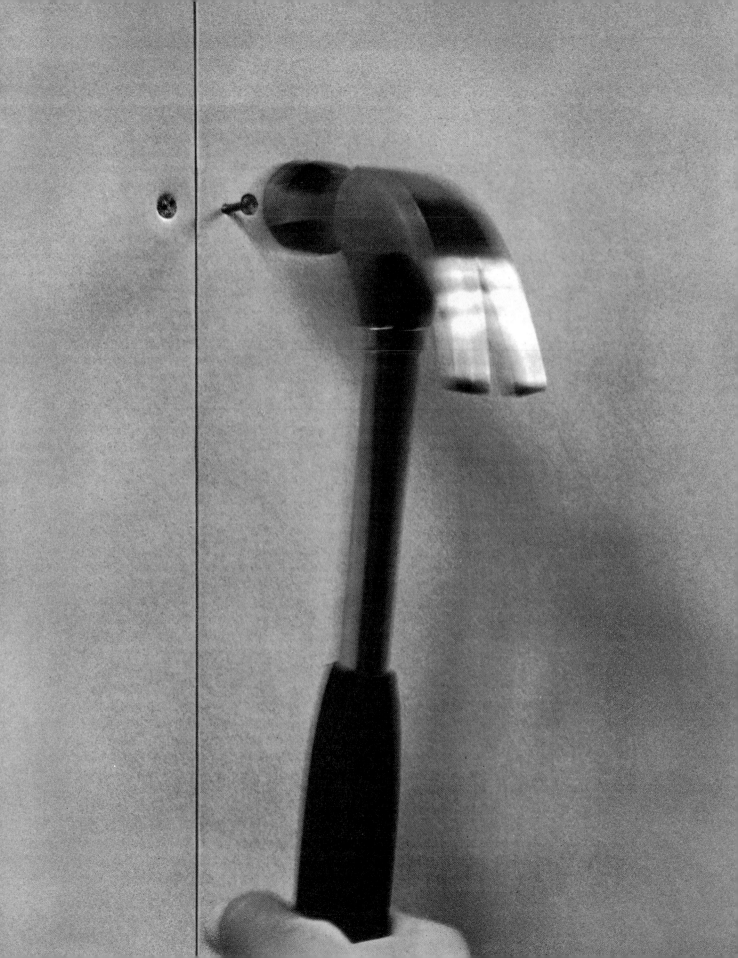

3

Putting Up and Tearing Down Walls

Double insurance. The timber studs that hold plasterboard may expand and contract as the house settles and temperature changes. Putting in the nails in pairs across a joint helps to ensure that the board is held rigid. Driving nails in a millimetre or so below the surface of the plasterboard with the last hammer blow sets them in so that they can be concealed with jointing compound to give the plasterboard a smooth finish.

Nothing transforms the interior of a house more dramatically than adding new walls or taking out old ones. Partitioning a living room can create an attractive front hall where none existed or turn a dining alcove into a fully-fledged room. Demolishing a partition can expand a living room by combining it with a little-used den. In many old homes an invitingly spacious living room can be created by removing the partition or doorway that separates lounge from dining room.

Putting up a wall is considerably simpler than most people imagine. The most common method is to install a partition wall of gypsum plasterboard panels fixed to a timber stud frame; the frame can be secured to the existing structure of the house. When you are adding such a wall, you construct the frame on the floor, where you can work comfortably; then you attach a nailing, or sole, plate to the floor and hang the frame above it like a huge wooden curtain *(pages 36–39)*. Providing a door is a simple matter of leaving an opening in the frame and installing a pre-hung unit *(pages 50–51)* after you finish the wall.

An alternative, which will provide better qualities of sound and heat insulation, is to build a wall from lightweight aggregate blocks, which are easily assembled using basic bricklaying skills *(pages 48–49)*.

Removing walls involves a number of additional considerations because some are load-bearing walls, that is, they carry some of the weight of the house. Non-loadbearing walls, whether of timber or masonry, can be treated as dispensable and can be removed fairly easily *(pages 57–58)*. Load-bearing walls, usually masonry, must be firmly propped during removal of any part of them, and you must install a supporting beam or lintel to support the opening *(pages 59–63)*.

All permanent partitions are attached to the structure of the house, and many of them hold electric wires, heating installations, and even plumbing pipes. Before you launch into adding or removing walls, analyse your house carefully. You can get the information you need with a little detective work. Tapping ceilings and walls helps to indicate basic construction, but the only sure way to learn what is where is to make small holes so that you can look inside the walls.

Before moving partitions, study family traffic patterns to avoid turning the main floor into an obstacle course or placing a door where it will block a window. Note the directions that windows face, so that you can preserve cross ventilation and natural lighting. If you have trouble visualizing the effect a new wall will have, approximate it roughly by hanging sheets from the ceiling, then consider the effect for a while. If your plans call for removing a wall, a dry run will be impossible and you will have to rely on accurate measurements and scale drawings to show how the space will change and how your furniture will fit into the new interior arrangement. Once you have decided on the changes you want to make, check to see if you need planning permission, and make sure that your scheme complies with local building regulations.

Techniques for Framing Partition Walls

Building a wall to divide an existing space is rather like hanging a curtain—a curtain made of wood. Like a curtain, the frame of the new wall goes into place not from the floor up, but from the ceiling down. Only in the last stage of assembly is the frame fastened to the floor.

In the simplest building methods, shown on these pages, most of the frame is assembled on the floor. It is lifted as a unit on to a beam called a sole plate which is fixed to the floor. Once upright, the frame is fastened in place by nails or screws driven through a second beam—the head plate—into the ceiling joists or concrete ceiling. The bottom of the assembly is then secured by nails driven through the sole plate.

For this final step, in which vertical beams called studs are nailed to the horizontal sole plate, you must master the knack of toenailing—that is, of fastening two pieces of timber together at a right angle by driving a nail through them at an angle of about 45 degrees. Toenailing a stud to a plate is easy after some practice, but at the beginning you may prefer to make a path for the toenails by drilling diagonal starter holes downwards through the stud and into the plate, using a bit slightly smaller than the nail.

In a room with concrete or masonry walls and ceilings, fix the partition frame to the existing structure using screws and plugs. For a timber ceiling, the new wall should ideally run either across the ceiling joists or under a single joist, so that the head plate can be nailed directly into a beam or beams above it. In a timber stud wall, the outermost stud of the new wall should lie directly against an existing stud, for easy stud-to-stud fastening. These ideal placements are not always practicable. When you must run a wall between joists or end it between studs, you will have to install short lengths of wood as nailing blocks between the joists or studs (opposite page, Step 3) to support the new wall.

Sometimes age and traffic will have caused the ceiling or the floor joists to sag. If this is the case, you may have to insert shims—short lengths or wedges of thin wood—between the head plate and the ceiling or between the sole plate and the floor to make sure that a plate is level and firm before nailing it in place.

When the frame is complete, install supporting pieces of wood—called noggings—between the studs to strengthen the frame and to provide nailing surfaces for the plasterboard. If nailing the plasterboard panels vertically (page 44), the noggings should be positioned half way between the floor and the ceiling; if the plasterboard is to be fixed horizontally (page 45), install noggings wherever two adjoining panels will butt up against each other.

The other decisions you must make when planning your partition wall will affect the interior and the sheathing of the wall frame. One has to do with electrical outlets. They can easily be installed in the open frame before the board is nailed on. Usually, power for the new outlets can be taken from an existing outlet box in a nearby house circuit, and the cable can be run through holes drilled through the new wall studs to new outlet boxes. Decide where you want your new outlets to be, and reinforce the position of switches on the frame with additional noggings (page 39, Step 8). You will also have to add supporting noggings where you plan to have a heavy fixture such as a washbasin or a kitchen cabinet and, if you are intending to tile the finished wall, the whole structure should be reinforced by further rows of noggings above and below the central one.

Standard 12.7 mm plasterboard has adequate soundproofing and insulation qualities for most domestic uses. This means, in practice, that in a quiet room such as a bedroom, normal conversation can be heard, but not understood, through the wall. To reduce the noise level further, the partition wall can be insulated with a double layer of plasterboard on each side, or by using lengths of glass fibre mat sandwiched between the studs and the two layers of plasterboard (page 44, below).

A Wall Built on the Floor, Tilted into Place

1 Marking the head and sole plates. Measure the length of the ceiling and floor where the new wall will run, and cut two 100 by 50s to this length for the head and sole plates. On the head plate, mark off areas 50 mm wide at each end for the two end studs. The distance between the intermediate studs depends on the thickness of the plasterboard you are using: for 9.5 mm board, space studs at 400 mm centres, and for 12.7 mm board, at 600 mm. The standard plasterboard width of 1200 mm conforms to both these spacings. Do not alter the position of the studs if the spacing does not work out evenly; instead, simply set the last two studs closer together. If you plan to have a door in the wall, mark the position of the door frame on the head plate. Set the head plate alongside the sole plate and transfer the markings, using a combination square to make sure that the markings line up.

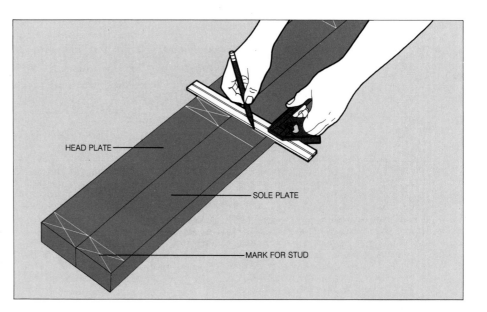

HEAD PLATE

SOLE PLATE

MARK FOR STUD

2 Assembling the frame. To determine the length of the studs, measure along a plumb line dropped from the ceiling to the floor at each end of the new wall and at one point in the middle—the three measurements should agree within a few millimetres. If they do not, measure each stud individually. Cut 100 by 50 mm studs 100 mm shorter than this measurement, to allow for the combined thicknesses of the head and sole plates. Set the head plate on its side on the floor, and nail the studs into place at the positions you have marked, using two 100 mm round-wire nails driven down through the top of the head plate to fasten each stud *(below)*.

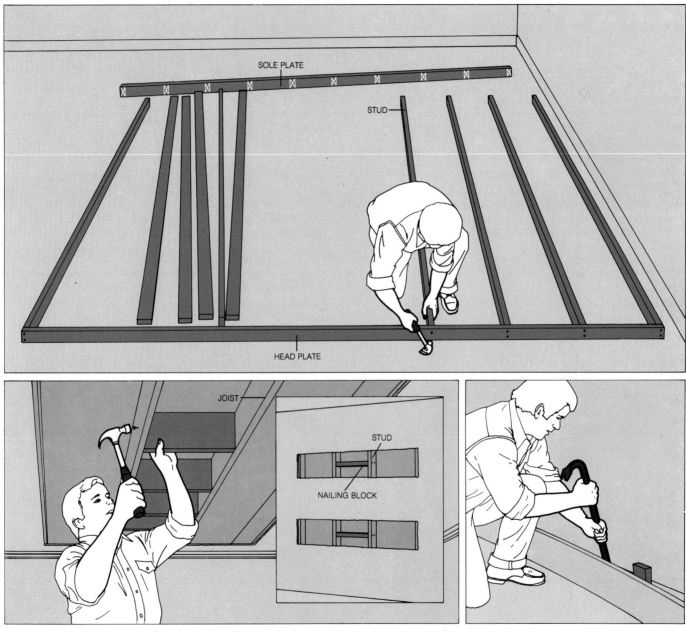

3 Finding or making frame supports. If the new wall is to be run across a number of joists, locate each joist *(page 10, Step 1)* and mark the ceiling at the joist positions. If the wall is to run parallel to the joists, try to position it directly under one joist. If the wall must run between two joists, install nailing blocks no more than 600 mm apart to support the frame. Cut the blocks from timber the same size as the joists, set the bottoms of the blocks flush to the bottoms of the joists and fasten each block with four 100 mm round-wire nails. If the space above the new wall is an unfloored attic, install the blocks from above; if not, cut out a strip of plasterboard wide enough to expose about half the edges of the flanking joists (the total width is usually 1200 mm). After installing the blocks, patch the strip with new plasterboard.

If the new wall meets an existing one between two studs *(inset)*, install 100 by 50 mm nailing blocks at about one-third and two-thirds of the distance from floor to ceiling. Cut two holes in the plasterboard to make the installation.

4 Preparing the existing wall. The new wall may meet an existing wall that is fitted with a skirting board at the floor and a moulding at the ceiling; for a tight fit, you must remove the skirting board, the quadrant strip (a narrow strip sometimes fastened at the bottom of the skirting board) and the moulding. Beginning at a corner or at the end of a strip, loosen the board, strip or moulding as much as you can without damaging it and insert a wooden wedge between it and the wall. Repeat the process, inserting wedges as you go, until it is completely detached.

5 **Installing the sole plate.** Drop a plumb line from the ceiling to the floor at each end of the line you have chosen for the head plate, and get a helper to mark the floor at these points; align the sole plate over the marks, butting it firmly against the existing wall. Fasten the sole plate to the floor at about 300 mm intervals, using 75 mm round-wire nails for a timber floor, or 75 mm No. 10 steel screws and plugs for a concrete floor.

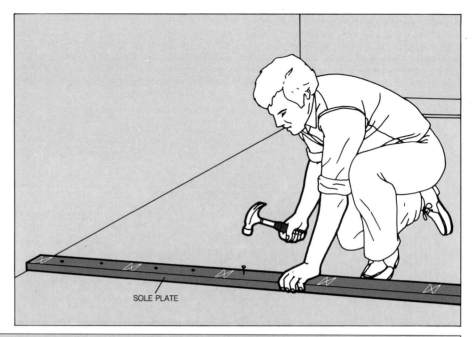

SOLE PLATE

6 **Hanging the frame.** With the aid of a helper, lift the assembled frame on to the sole plate and hold it against the ceiling and the existing wall in the position you have chosen for it. While your helper holds the frame in place, fasten the ends of the head plate to the joists or nailing blocks in the ceiling with 100 mm round-wire nails, or with 75 mm No. 10 screws and plugs for a con-crete ceiling. Nail or screw the outermost studs of the new wall to the existing one, then nail or screw the rest of the head plate to the joists or ceiling. Pack any gaps between the floor or the ceiling with wooden shims (*page 12, top left*).

HEAD PLATE

7 **Toenailing the studs.** Set the bottoms of the studs directly over the sole plate marks: use a spirit level to be sure the studs are absolutely vertical. Toenail the studs to the sole plate, using three 100 mm round-wire nails per stud—two on one side and the third centred on the other, so that the nails do not meet.

SOLE PLATE

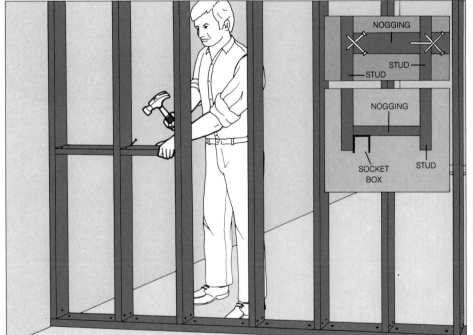

NOGGING

STUD

STUD

NOGGING

SOCKET BOX

STUD

WALL EXTENSION

8 **Installing noggings.** Decide the height that you want the noggings to be, and mark each stud this distance from the ground. Measure the distance between the first and second studs, and cut a 100 by 50 mm nogging to fit exactly between them. Hold the nogging between the studs at the position you have marked and toenail the nogging into the stud against the wall. Nail through the back of the second stud into the other end of the nogging. Then measure the distance between the second and third studs, and cut a nogging to fit. Toenail from above and below the nogging into the second stud as before *(top inset)*, and nail through the back of the third stud into the other end. Repeat for all the noggings, cutting, levelling and fixing each one individually.

To support an electric switch or socket box, turn the nogging on its side between the studs, as shown in a plan view in the bottom inset. Position the nogging so that when the socket box is screwed to the nogging it will lie flush with the face of the plasterboard.

9 **Turning a corner.** In a wall that turns at a right angle, reinforce the corner to make a firm attachment for the wall extension and its covering plasterboard. Install an additional stud 50 mm back from the stud at the corner; this stud can be put in when the frame is assembled on the floor or toenailed in place after the assembly is hung. Using nails driven through the studs, fasten two 100 by 50 mm nailing blocks, each cut to a length of 50 mm, between the studs at points one-third and two-thirds of the distance from the floor to the ceiling. Use the blocks like nailing blocks in an existing wall *(page 37, Step 3)* to secure the new wall extension.

A Place for a Door in a Stud Wall

For an opening in a new partition—used as an open passageway between two rooms or closed off with a door—one or more regular wall studs must be eliminated. In their place is built a rigid supporting structure called a rough doorframe.

For a door, the rough frame must be built to an exact width and height based on the dimensions of the door and its lining. Buy a door set *(page 50)* from a builders' merchant before framing the opening, so you can make precise calculations beforehand *(below)*. If you plan to finish the rough opening with plasterboard as an open passageway, you can dispense with these calculations.

Remember that the best position for new light switches and electric points in a new wall is next to a doorway on the side of the frame away from the hinges. Decide on the location of these fittings, and install supporting noggings *(page 39)* before fixing the plasterboard.

A rough frame for a door. A doorway is framed into a new partition between two outer studs, each reinforced with additional studs nailed to the inside. The top of the frame is formed by a short crosspiece, called a header, which is toe-nailed *(page 39)* between the reinforcing studs. Short studs called cripple studs fixed between the header and the head plate provide a surface for nailing plasterboard over the door.

Start the rough frame by installing two ordinary wall studs *(page 37)* far enough apart for all the components of the door and frame: the door set, two 50 mm-wide reinforcing studs and 6 mm all round for packing. Fit noggings for electrical fixtures *(page 39, Step 8)* and complete the rough doorframe as shown on the right. Finish the partition with two plasterboard sheets the full length of the partition, plus a separate piece nailed to the head plate, header and cripple studs.

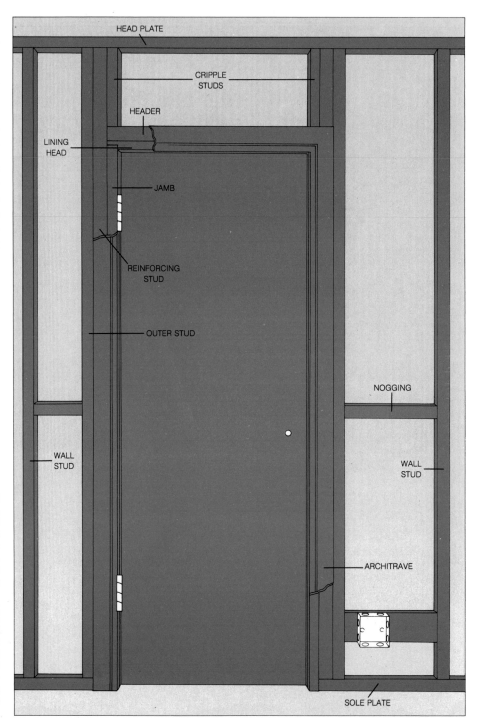

HEAD PLATE

CRIPPLE STUDS

HEADER

LINING HEAD

JAMB

REINFORCING STUD

OUTER STUD

NOGGING

WALL STUD

WALL STUD

ARCHITRAVE

SOLE PLATE

1 Reinforcing the studs. Lay the reinforcing studs against the inside of each outer stud. Bracing the outer stud with your foot, lean over and nail the second stud at 400 mm intervals, using 100 mm round-wire nails.

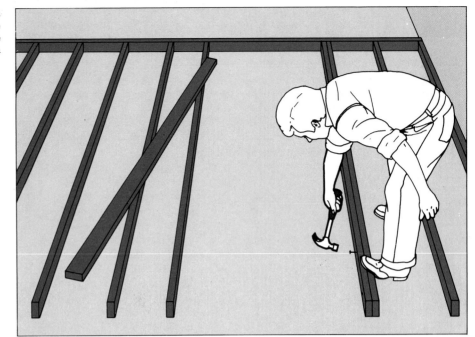

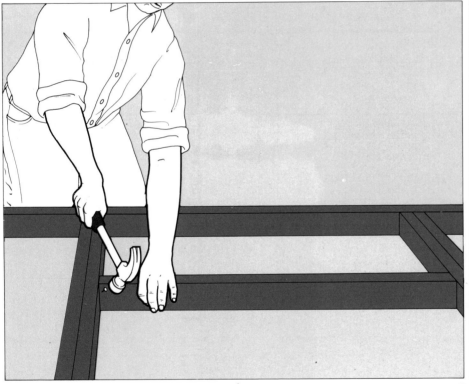

2 Installing the header. Cut a 100 by 50 mm header to fit between the reinforcing studs. Place it in position allowing for 6 mm of packing above the door, and toenail it to the studs at each end from above and below, using 100 mm round-wire nails.

3 Installing the cripple studs. Cut cripple studs long enough to extend from the top of the header to the head plate. Nail the cripple studs to the reinforcing studs using 100 mm round-wire nails.

To complete the rough doorframe after raising the wall into place *(page 38)* cut away the section of sole plate from between the insides of the two reinforcing studs.

The Professional's Way with Plasterboard

Plasterboard is the common-sense solution for sheathing interior walls—much less costly, and easier to install, than wet plaster trowelled over wood and metal lath. It is made of gypsum plaster pressed into a sandwich, usually 9.5 or 12.7 mm thick, 1200 mm wide and 1800 or 2400 mm long, with a layer of ivory-coloured paper on the front, and heavy grey paper on the back.

The resulting sheet is not particularly strong: it breaks if you bend it enough, and its corners crumble if the sheet is dropped. A stout hammer blow will punch right through it. But you can nail through it cleanly, break it neatly and quickly along a scored line, and saw it rapidly with a wood saw. It will hold a hook strongly enough to hang light pictures, and it readily takes anchors of various types. If you have to cut into plasterboard, you can patch it to its original smoothness, and it makes a good match for existing smooth plaster.

Making smooth joints to hide the seams between sheets takes practice. Using plasterboard that has a slight bevel along the long edges makes the job easier. Adjacent bevels are filled in with jointing compound—supplied as a powder, to which you add water—and then reinforced by paper covering tape 50 mm wide. Outside corners are strengthened with angled metal strips called angle bead.

The jointing compound is spread and feathered out with tools made especially for the task. You will need a 200 mm jointing applicator, for applying and feathering the compound, a taping knife for embedding the tape, and a sponge for smoothing each application (*pages 46–47*).

Plasterboard is put up on walls after the ceiling (also, these days, usually made of plasterboard) is finished. Fix plasterboards vertically (*page 44*) on walls which are up to 2400 mm high; this is the easiest method for one person, and gives a smooth surface with the minimum number of joints. For walls which are higher than this, fix the panels horizontally, as it is easier to conceal joints at the bevelled edges of a plasterboard panel than joints cut across it.

Installing plasterboard on a sloping wall, such as under a staircase or in an attic, is a more complex operation, but the basic techniques are the same. The method used is shown on page 76.

If the board is to be nailed vertically, estimate your needs by measuring the perimeter of the room, dividing the total by 1200 mm, and rounding up to the nearest whole sheet. To install plasterboard horizontally, treat each wall separately in making measurements.

In rooms which require additional qualities of heat or sound insulation, or protection from moisture, specially adapted types of plasterboard can be substituted for the standard grades. However, you can also achieve good levels of draught and sound-proofing by fixing glass fibre mat or slabs between the studs after the first sheet of plasterboard has been nailed in place (*page 44*). Avoid using polystyrene or polyurethane insulating materials, as they create a fire hazard if they come into contact with faulty wiring installations.

Cutting the Sheets

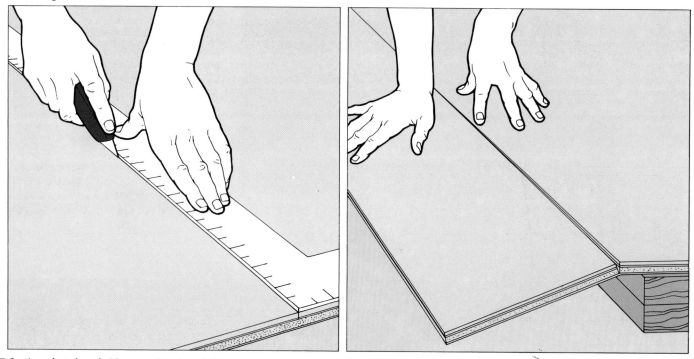

1 **Scoring plasterboard.** Measure the size of the sheet needed and mark the face—ivory side—accordingly, using a steel square and pressing hard with the pencil to indent the surface. Score the pencil line with a trimming knife.

2 **Snapping the core.** Place two 100 by 50 mm off-cuts under the board just behind the scored line. Press down on the waste end of the sheet, snapping the core. Finish by slicing through the backing paper with a trimming knife.

3 **Measuring for cutouts.** Cut holes for fixtures that will protrude through the plasterboard before setting it in place. Measure the distance from the ceiling to the top and bottom of the fixture. Record the measurements on the face side of the board with pencil marks. Next measure the width of the cutout—the distance from the corner, or the adjacent fastened sheet, to both edges of the fixture—and make corresponding marks. Connect the marks to outline the hole.

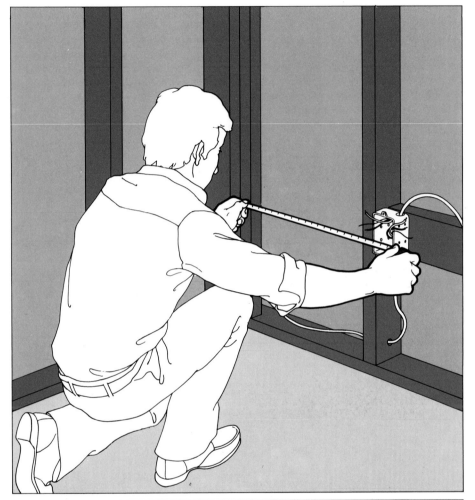

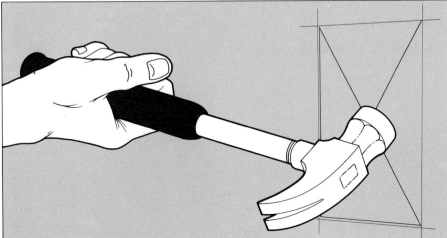

Tips for a Smooth Job

☐ Stack and store plasterboard flat; if it leans it may bend or break.

☐ When storing plasterboard out of doors, or on a concrete floor, stack the boards on top of three or four pieces of scrap timber, in order to protect them from moisture.

☐ Cut plasterboard short instead of long to fit into a given space. The skirting board will cover up to 40 mm of space at the bottom of the board. Trying to force plasterboard into too small a space crumbles the edges.

☐ Be sure you get plasterboard with bevelled edges for ease in finishing the joints with jointing tape and compound.

☐ Pre-mixed jointing compound is easier to work with than the dry form because it always has the same consistency and it will retain its moisture content for a year after first being opened and resealed.

☐ Applying plasterboard horizontally gives you the advantage of fewer joints to finish although the weight of longer lengths makes placing it a two-person job. It is the best method for high-ceilinged rooms and halls, where vertical joints are more noticeable.

☐ Take safety precautions when you are working with dried jointing compound, whether sanding new compound or removing old. Wear a face mask, goggles and hat to keep the dust out of lungs, eyes and hair.

4 **Cutting for fixtures.** Score along the pencil marks on the face of the plasterboard with a trimming knife. Make additional scores joining up opposite corners of the shape, and complete the cutout by hitting sharply with a hammer in the centre of the outline *(left)*. Trim off the waste pieces of plasterboard by cutting through the backing paper.

Installing the Sheets

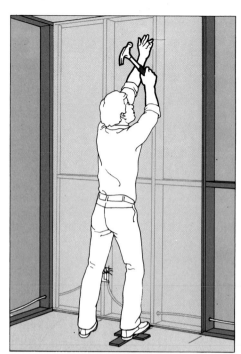

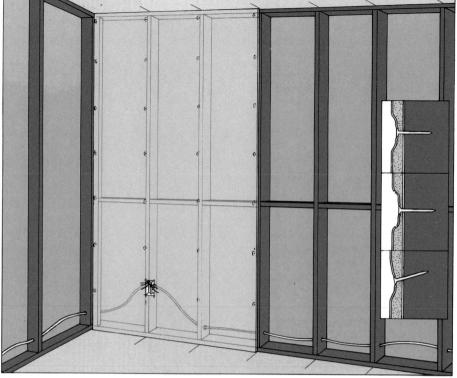

1 Positioning the board. Mark the stud centres on the ceiling and floor. Lean the first sheet into position in a corner. Put a wooden offcut under it, slide a second offcut under the first, and use them as a foot-operated lever and fulcrum to hold the sheet up against the ceiling. Align the edge away from the corner with the centre of a stud and, using the ceiling marks as a guide, drive a plasterboard nail into each stud, 300 mm down from the ceiling. These will hold the sheet in place, so release the lever.

2 Nailing the board. Starting at the top, drive nails into each stud and nogging at intervals of about 200 mm. At seams, nail 9 mm in from the edges. Between the edges, use the marks on the floor and ceiling to help nail into studs you cannot see. If you miss, pull out the nail and try again; jointing compound will later fill the hole. Drive each nail flush, then hammer again to set it a millimetre or so below the surface *(top inset)*. Be careful not to make this blow so hard that you break the paper covering *(centre inset)*, or hit the nail at an angle with the same result *(bottom inset)*. Dimpling the nails allows the heads to be covered with jointing compound and hidden.

Insulating a Partition Wall

Fitting insulation material. This should be done before the second side of the frame is sheathed with plasterboard. For a timber stud partition, use 60 or 100 mm paper-faced glass fibre or rock-wool mat, which is manufactured to fit both 400 and 600 mm stud spacing. Wearing gloves, mask and goggles, cut a length of mat to fit between the studs and noggings, and make cutouts to fit round any electrical installations.

The paper facing has a 38 mm overlap on each edge of the mat; staple this to the studs *(right)*.

A Horizontal Pattern for Special Cases

Putting up the board. Mark the stud positions on the ceiling and floor. Drive 65 mm round-wire nails far enough into the studs to take the weight of the board along the line of the noggings. With a helper, lift the plasterboard so that it butts against the ceiling, resting on the nails. If the ceiling is uneven, scribe the plasterboard to fit exactly, using compasses as described in Step 3 on page 9. Secure the plasterboard by nailing it to the studs about 300 mm from the ceiling, then finish nailing to the studs and noggings (*Step 2, opposite*) and remove the 65 mm nails. If the wall is more than 2400 mm high, put up a second sheet in the same way.

Before putting up the bottom sheet, measure from the bottom of the last installed sheet to the floor at each end. Mark these distances on the new sheet, snap a chalk line between the marks, then score and break the sheet (*page 42, Step 1*). With a helper, raise the plasterboard—using two fulcrums and levers—and nail in place. Cover any unevenness at the base of the wall by installing skirting board (*pages 52–55*).

Making Repairs with Plasterboard

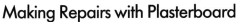

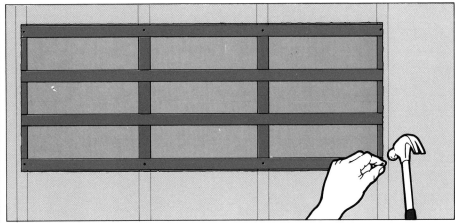

Replacing sections of plasterboard. Cut new sheets to fit the opening and nail them after straightening the existing edges and cleaning off any bits of tape or jointing compound. If you made the opening by cutting along stud edges, provide nailing surfaces for the plasterboard by nailing pieces of 50 by 25 mm timber inside the end studs, to be flush with the stud surfaces. For a small hole, extend the edges to the nearest studs and put up 50 by 25 mm nailing strips.

Replacing plaster with plasterboard. Wearing a mask, goggles and hat, extend the opening to the centres of the nearest studs with a chisel. Then straighten the top and bottom edges with a keyhole saw. Remove the lath (using tin snips to cut wire lath). To make the surface of the plasterboard patch flush with the plaster surface, nail strips of new lath across the studs at the top and bottom of the opening and at 400 mm intervals in between (*above*), shimming them as necessary. Mark the positions of the new nailing surfaces on the plaster wall. Alternatively, if the studs are in line and no shimming is needed, nail a scrap of 7 mm plywood, cut to the size of the hole, across the opening. Cut the plasterboard to fit the hole and nail it (*Step 2, opposite*).

Concealing the Joints

1 **Applying jointing compound to seams.** Using a 200 mm jointing applicator, spread jointing compound like butter to fill the trough formed by the bevelled edges of the plasterboard, with a layer covering the adjacent surface approximately 1 mm deep *(right)*. (To fill joints at corners, follow the instructions on the opposite page.) Then run the applicator down the joint in one motion, to smooth out the compound. Wipe the applicator frequently, otherwise the compound will harden on it and score grooves in the wet compound.

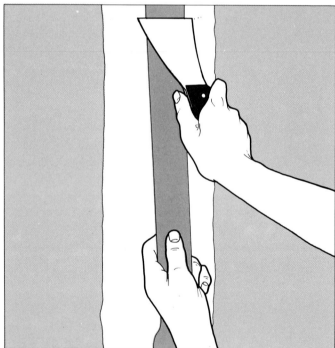

2 **Taping the joint.** Cut the length of tape needed to fill the joint. With your finger, press one end of the jointing tape into the wet compound at the top of the joint. Keep the tape straight with one hand and use the other hand to embed the tape in the jointing compound with a 100 mm taping knife. Watch for air pockets and wrinkles in the tape; if they appear, lift the tape, pull it tight, and embed it again. If the tape is badly wrinkled, peel it up and tear it off the damaged section. Start again with fresh tape, positioning the ends of the sections as close together as possible.

3 **Feathering the joint.** As the tape is embedded, compound will squeeze out along the sides of the joint. Run the taping knife down each side, spreading the compound outwards. Press hardest on the outside edge of the knife so the compound gradually spreads to a feathered edge. Apply jointing compound to the nail dimples on the intermediate studs, feathering the edges. A day later, apply a second coat to the joints with a 200 mm jointing applicator. Use a sponge to feather the compound about 250 mm on either side of the joint. After another day, apply a third layer of jointing compound, thinned with water if necessary to make it spread evenly, and feathered just beyond the 250 mm line.

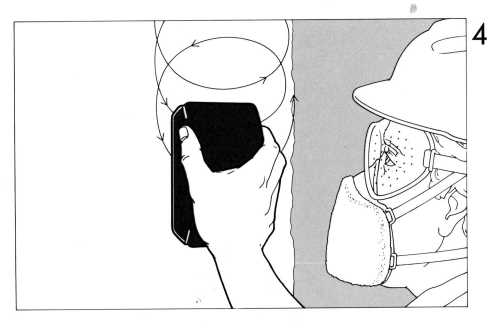

4 **Smoothing the surface.** When the last coat of compound is completely dry, smooth the surface with fine glass paper on a sanding block, working in a circular motion from top to bottom; take care not to sand the paper tape. Similarly, sand over the filled-in nail dimples. Caution: much dust is generated during this process. Wear protective goggles, mask and hat, and keep the working area well ventilated.

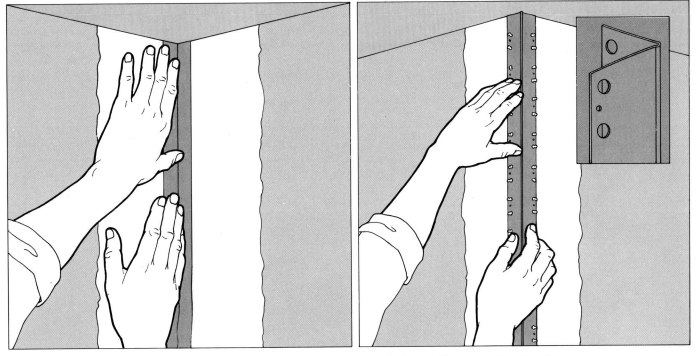

Taping inside corners. Use the taping knife to spread jointing compound thickly in the crack in the inside corner of a wall or between a wall and the ceiling. Run the knife along each side of the joint to smooth the compound. Using one 600 to 900 mm-long strip at a time, fold the paper tape in half along its length. Press the crease lightly into the corner by running your fingers along the joint (above). Draw the knife along each side of the joint, embedding the paper and feathering the edges. When applying the second and third coats, do one side at a time. Leave the compound to dry for one day between coats.

Strengthening outside corners. Spread a 3 mm-deep layer of compound about 50 mm wide over both sides of the corner. Press a reinforcing strip of corner tape or metal angle bead (inset) into the compound so it fits flat on each side—you can nail the metal bead if you want to, but it should stick without nailing. Run the taping knife from ceiling to floor, smoothing out the compound that oozes out at the sides of the tape or through the metal bead perforations, and feathering with a sponge. Apply two more coats of compound at one-day intervals. When completed, the rounded tip of the metal bead will still show but will be covered by the wall finish.

A Lightweight Block Partition for a Timber or Concrete Floor

Building blocks make an ideal alternative to a plasterboard-clad timber frame for an interior non-loadbearing wall. They are lightweight, durable and easy to assemble with a minimum of bricklaying skill.

Building blocks come in a variety of sizes and weights, but only two types are light enough for a partition wall. Aerated aggregate blocks, which are made from pottery dust, clinker or fuel ash, are the lightest and easiest to use, and also provide excellent insulation against noise and heat loss. Breeze blocks, made from the same materials, are also suitable but are heavier, and can only be used on a concrete floor.

Standard blocks are based on a modular unit of 450 by 225 mm: this is a nominal size and includes an allowance of 10 mm all round for the mortar joint. For interior walls, choose a thickness of 75 or 100 mm. To estimate the number of blocks you will need, allow 10 blocks per square metre of wall, plus 10 per cent for wastage. Store the blocks in a dry place; damp blocks will increase the drying time of your wall.

To level the floor, lay a timber sole plate the same length and width as the proposed partition; install vertical battens at each end as a guide for the blocks. Lay the blocks in a half-lap bond, as illustrated opposite. Plan the location of any openings in the wall: the construction will be much easier if you position a door so that it lies a distance of a block and a half, or multiples thereof, from the end of the wall. Estimate the number of half blocks you will need, and cut them before you start, using an old handsaw or bolster and chisel.

The mortar should combine five parts soft building sand to one part cement, and approximately half a litre of water per kilogram of sand and cement. The exact amount of water needed will depend on temperature and humidity. The consistency of the mortar should be that of soft butter—if it is too dry, it will not form a strong bond. Slightly wetter mortar is easier to work, and the blocks will absorb any extra moisture. About 40 kilograms of sand will make enough mortar for about 20 blocks and a sole plate—don't mix any more than this because it only remains workable for about an hour.

Build up to five courses in a day; more than this may cause the wall to buckle. If using breeze blocks in a high-ceilinged room where there will be more than two block courses above the doorframe, you must provide extra support for the blocks. A galvanized steel lintel, available in standard lengths to cover most doorways plus the necessary overlap into the blocks on either side, can be mortared into the wall before the doorframe is installed.

You should be able to build an average height partition wall and install a door set in two days. Leave the wall two more days to dry before electrical installations are made. Cover wires with plastic or galvanized conduits, held in place by cable clips, before the wall is plastered. Fix skirtings to the completed wall using cut nails.

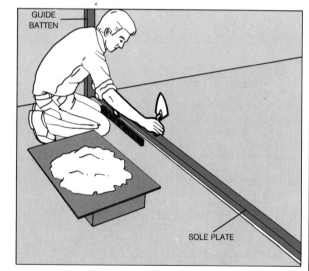

1 **Laying the sole plate.** Tack guide battens to the existing walls at each end of the proposed new wall; use a level to check they are vertical. Cut a 75 by 50 mm or 100 by 50 mm sole plate the length of the new wall, lay it on the floor beside the battens, and trace its position on the floor. Remove the sole plate and, using a bricklayer's trowel, place slices of mortar between the lines. Run the trowel point down the centre of the mortar, making a furrow to distribute the mortar evenly under the sole plate. Place the plate on the mortar and tap it down with the trowel handle *(above)*, or a lump hammer if the mortar is too dry. Check level, and adjust the plate by tapping with the trowel. Scrape off excess mortar.

2 **Positioning the doorway.** Use dry blocks to gauge the position of the doorway, and mark it on the sole plate. The space allowed should include the width of your door set, plus 6 mm all round. Calculate the number of blocks you will need for five courses, and cut any half blocks you will need.

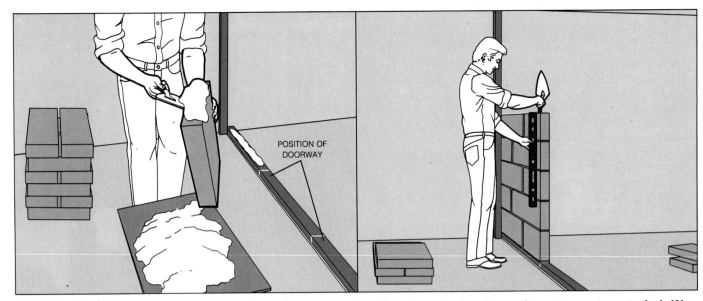

POSITION OF DOORWAY

3 **Building up to the doorframe.** Starting with the shortest section of partition, mortar the sole plate between the wall and the doorframe. Take a whole block, and spread a slice of mortar approximately 10 mm thick on the end which will touch the wall *(above, left)*. Bed the block on the sole plate, butting it up firmly against the wall, and tap it into place. Mortar the second block at one end, and push it up against the first. Scrape away any excess mortar, and check that the blocks are level and vertical. Build the wall up to five courses in this way, using half blocks at the start of every alternate course to create the half-lap bond, and checking that each course is level and plumb as you go. Leave until the following day, then continue building up to the nearest course below the height of the doorframe. Build the wall the other side of the doorframe in the same way.

4 **Installing the doorframe.** Cut away the sole plate between the doorframe marks and chisel away the mortar. Lift the frame into position, check for level *(above)*, planing the bottom of one side if necessary, and tack it to the sole plate on either side. Nail or screw into the blocks using 100 mm cut nails, or 75 mm No. 10 steel screws.

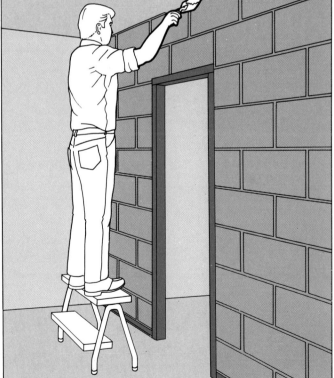

5 **Finishing the wall.** Build up the rest of the wall, trimming blocks to fit round the doorframe and to make a level course over the door. If necessary, cut blocks lengthways for the last course, leaving a gap of up to 12 mm above it. Press mortar into this gap, using the underside of the trowel, to complete the wall *(above)*.

A Door Set, Ready to Nail In

Time was when apprentice carpenters got out of bed slowly to face the task of finishing a doorframe and hanging the door. The craftsman had to erect a plumb and square lining, the frame in which a door hangs; add a doorstop, the strip round the inside of the frame that prevents the door from swinging too far through the opening when closing; mortise recesses for the door hinges; then fasten the door itself in position. Finally, he would attach the architrave, the decorative trim that frames the lining and hides the ragged edges of plaster or plasterboard round the door opening.

Fortunately, much of this work can now be eliminated by installing a factory-made door set. This is supplied complete with pre-cut door lining and a ready-fitted doorstop, hinges and keep plate; even the architraves are already mitred.

Put up a door set after plasterboard has been installed *(pages 42–47)* or plaster has dried, but before the floor covering is laid *(pages 70–73)* and the room is trimmed *(pages 52–55)*. But before you commence work, you must decide whether you want the finished door to open to the left or the right, and install the lining accordingly.

To erect the lining, first assemble the head and jambs, then place the lining in the door opening. Checking for squareness, insert packing if necessary, and nail the assembly to the doorframe.

The flush door comes either pre-primed, or in a range of veneer finishes. The height of a standard door is 1981 mm and there are three standard door widths; 610 mm, 686 mm, and 762 mm. The door linings vary in depth: a 108 mm-deep lining is suitable for a 75 mm block partition wall *(pages 48–49)*; for a wider 100 mm timber stud wall lined with sheets of plasterboard, use a 120 mm door lining.

The hinges come already attached to the door lining. To hang the door, take out the pins that hold the two halves of the hinge together, and screw the loose hinge leaves to the recesses that are mortised in the door. Place the door in the lining, and fit the hinges back together again with the hinge pins. If necessary, adjust the position of the keep plate, to ensure that the door opens and closes smoothly.

Finish the installation by nailing the three pieces of ready-mitred architrave—the head first, then the side pieces—round the doorframe. Pre-hung doors come with holes already drilled to accommodate a standard set of handles.

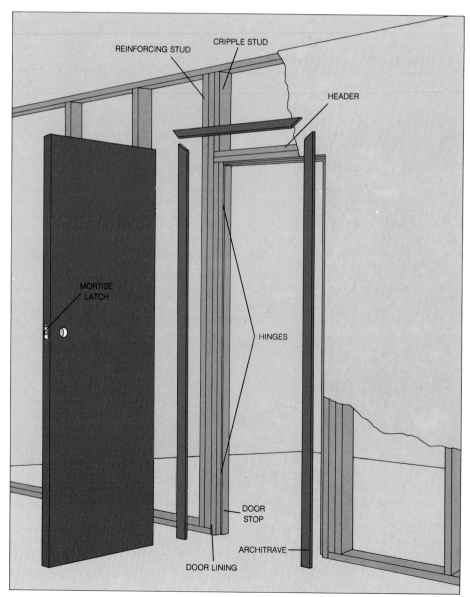

A door set. This factory-made unit consists of a door with ready-cut hinge recesses and a fitted mortise latch; a door lining with a doorstop and hinges attached to one jamb, and the keep plate to the other; and pre-cut and mitred architrave sections. The door set can be fitted to open to the right or the left, and into or out of a room.

1 **Assembling and positioning the door lining.** Lay the three sections of the lining in position on the floor. Align the doorstops and the half-lap joint of the head and right-hand jamb, and fix them together using 75 mm round-wire nails *(inset)*. Nail the left-hand jamb to the head in the same way. Tack a 50 by 25 mm piece of timber between the two jambs at the bottom of the frame to keep them parallel while installing the door *(right)*. Raise the assembled lining into the doorway, and centre it carefully. Check that it is plumb and square, and that the lining head is level.

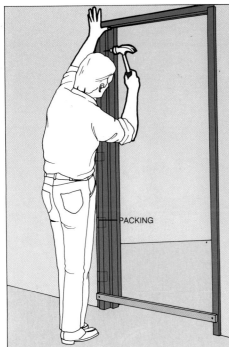

PACKING

2 **Fixing the lining to the wall.** Pack the lining with pieces of plywood at the points where it will be nailed to the walls. Check that the sides are plumb. Fix the lining to the reinforcing studs *(page 40)*, starting with the hinge jamb; use 63 mm lost-head nails for wooden studs, and 63 mm No. 8 screws for masonry. Remove the brace and check again that the head is level, and make adjustments if necessary.

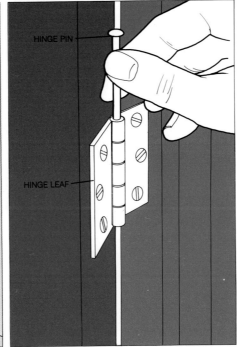

HINGE PIN

HINGE LEAF

3 **Hanging the door.** Release the door section of the hinges by taking out the pins; screw each section of hinge into the ready-cut recesses in the door. Place the door in the opening, supporting it on a shim, match up the leaves of the hinges and replace the pins. Adjust the keep plate if the door does not close smoothly.

4 **Fitting the architraves.** Centre the head of the architrave over the door. Check that it is level, and secure it with 37 mm oval nails, starting 75 mm from one corner. Repeat at the other corner, then nail at 150 mm intervals in between. Hold each of the uprights in position, and check they will fit; plane the bottoms if necessary. Nail the uprights to the frame, making sure that they are butted up against the mitred ends of the head to form neat corners. Finish by nailing vertically downwards through each corner. Repeat for the other side of the door.

A Neat Finish for a New Wall

Skirting board adds a finishing touch to a room, and also covers up ragged plasterboard ends and gaps between the flooring and the wall. In many rooms, particularly those with high ceilings, ceiling moulding fulfils a similar function at the corner between wall and ceiling.

Install skirting board and ceiling moulding after you have finished work on the walls, ceiling and floor, but before painting or laying any floor covering. The quadrant moulding, a strip which seals the joint between the skirting board and the floor, is installed last of all.

Skirting board made of timber or plastic is sold in random lengths. Ceiling moulding made of plasterboard, polystyrene or timber is available in 1800 or 2400 mm lengths. Fit skirting or moulding to walls in order of size, starting with the longest wall, and try to cut the pieces so that you only have to make one joint along each wall except the last.

For exterior corners, cut both pieces of skirting using a mitre box (right); for interior corners, cut one piece flush with the wall, and scribe the second piece to fit over it (opposite page, top left). If you have to make a join in the middle of a wall, lap two mitred pieces of board over one another (box, opposite page).

To estimate the quantity of skirting or moulding you need to buy, measure each wall individually, and add 50 mm for each angle to be cut at the ends, remembering that skirting is butted square against the architrave of a door.

How to Cut Corners

Mitring skirting board. To cut skirting board to fit an exterior corner, butt the board against the wall in its final position and mark the position of the corner straight across the top of the board (inset). Without covering the mark, press a strip of masking tape down the back of the board, along the line of the cut, in order to prevent splintering. Set the saw guide of a mitre box at a 45-degree angle and position the skirting board in the box so that the wall side of the board, when cut, will be shorter than the front side. Cut the skirting board from right to left for the left-hand side of the corner, and from left to right for the right-hand side of the corner.

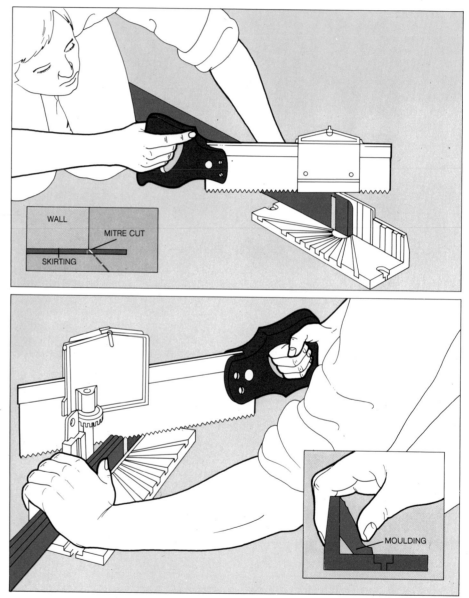

WALL

MITRE CUT

SKIRTING

MOULDING

Mitring ceiling moulding. To cut ceiling moulding for an exterior corner, mark the guideline on the bottom edge of the moulding. Place the moulding upside down in the mitre box, that is with the guideline upwards and with the moulding's two flat surfaces against the side and bottom of the mitre box. As with skirting board, cut so the wall side is shorter than the face side for an exterior corner. Since the moulding is upside down in the mitre box, cut from right to left for the right-hand side of an exterior corner and from left to right for the left-hand side.

Making Corners Fit Exactly

Scribing interior corners. To fit skirting to interior corners, cut one piece of skirting to fit the exact distance between two walls. Mitre the other piece as for an exterior corner *(opposite page, above)*, then cut along the profile to fit over the first piece using a coping saw or keyhole saw held at right angles to the skirting.

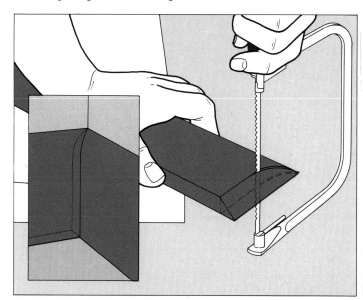

A Mid-Wall Skirting Joint

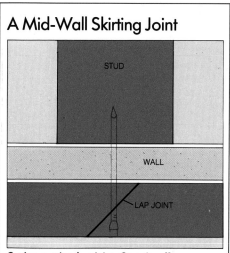

Cutting a mitre-lap joint. Occasionally you may have to splice two lengths of skirting or ceiling moulding. For a stud wall, locate a stud near the point where you want to splice. Mark the top of the skirting at the centre of the stud and mitre it at a 45-degree angle with the skirting positioned so that the cut bisects the mark. Then mitre another piece of skirting at the same angle but in the opposite direction. Butt the angled cuts together against the wall. For a stud wall, drive a 40 mm nail through the spliced ends into the centre of the stud. For a plaster-brick or block wall, drive 40 mm cut nails directly into the masonry. Paint will hide the splice, but stain will not, so avoid splicing if you plan to stain or varnish.

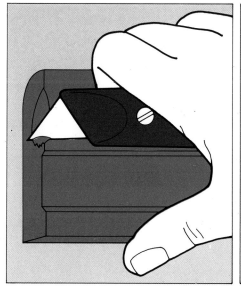

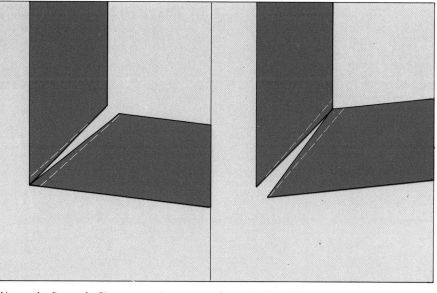

Feathering angles for plastic skirting. To ease the fit of plastic skirting at exterior corners, cut a crescent-shaped piece out of the angle-sawed end of the skirting with a trimming knife or coping saw. Begin the cut 12 mm below the top of the skirting; cutting out any portion of the top will create a visible gap in the joint. Cut inwards and down to the bottom *(above)*.

Making angles fit exactly. Since corners in a room seldom make perfect 90-degree angles, the angles of mitred skirting joints must usually be widened or narrowed to fit corners perfectly before the skirting is finally nailed in place. If the joint gapes on the wall side *(above, left)* increase the angle formed by the two strips of skirting board by shaving away the fronts of the angled cuts with a trimming knife, checking the fit frequently. If the joint gapes on the face side *(above, right)*, decrease the angle by shaving away the back portions of the cuts.

The Right Way to Fix Skirting and Moulding

Fasten skirting board and moulding with the same care used in cutting or correcting angles. The strips can pull away from the wall if they are incorrectly nailed, and a misplaced hammer blow can easily dent soft timber, plasterboard or polystyrene.

After making sure that the joints are properly fitted (page 53) begin nailing a strip of skirting board at one corner, and continue across the room to the opposite end. If the wall is longer than your skirting, or if the length of a strip of skirting board proves unwieldy, cut and splice as described on page 53. Remove any irregularities on the wall—such as accretions of paint or lumps of jointing compound from newly installed plasterboard—to ensure a close fit. Before finishing, punch the nails about 3 mm into the wood and fill the holes with wood filler. Fit plasterboard or polystyrene ceiling moulding in the same way, and glue it in place using the adhesive recommended by the manufacturer.

Fastening skirting board. For a stud wall, fix skirting to the wall by driving two 65 mm lost-head nails into the board at each corner, and at each wall stud. Drive one nail through the middle of the board straight into the stud, and the other at a 45-degree angle into the sole plate near the bottom of the skirting (inset). For a masonry wall, attach skirting with 65 mm cut nails, or 50 mm No. 8 screws and plugs.

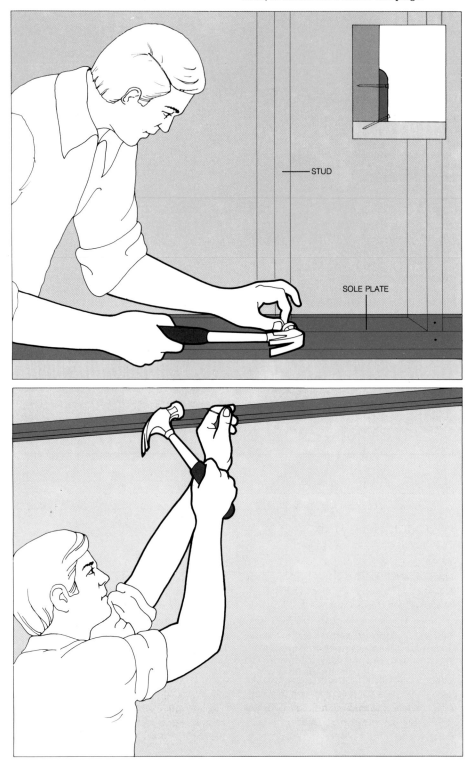

STUD

SOLE PLATE

Fastening ceiling moulding. Attach plasterboard or polystyrene ceiling moulding using a recommended adhesive to fix it to both wall and ceiling. Hold plasterboard moulding in place with panel pins while the adhesive sets; dress-making pins can be used in the same way for polystyrene moulding. Nail wooden ceiling moulding using 65 mm lost-head nails for a timber wall, or cut nails for a masonry wall.

Finishing mitred corners. Hold the mitred ends of two strips of skirting firmly together by driving 40 mm lost-head nails through the skirting into the wall close to the corner. For skirting board and ceiling mouldings, drive two nails at each side of the corner; for quadrant moulding, drive one nail into the skirting board at each side.

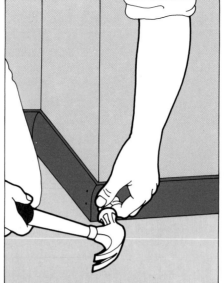

Fastening quadrant moulding. Nail the quadrant strip to the floor with panel pins at intervals of approximately 300 mm. Drive the nail at a 45-degree angle downwards into the floor just above the middle of the strip; nailing too near the top can split the wood.

Fitting quadrant moulding to doorways. To improve the appearance of the quadrant strip where it juts into the room past the architrave of a door, bookcase or other built-in, sculpt the obtrusive end into a curve. Holding the strip in place, mark a freehand line on the strip. Begin the line at the point where the quadrant strip protrudes past the frame, and curve the line away from the frame. Set the quadrant strip on a solid surface, cut along the line and sand it smooth.

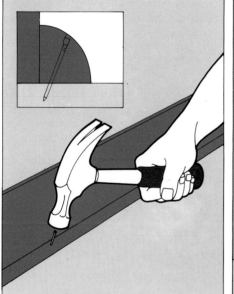

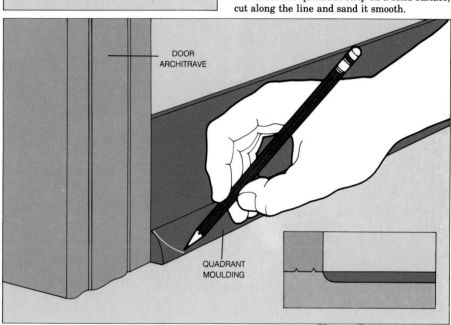

DOOR ARCHITRAVE

QUADRANT MOULDING

Marrying New Trim to Old

When you add a partition to a room you may be able to buy new skirting that matches. If so, set your mitre box at a 45-degree angle and saw enough of the old skirting, already removed from the wall, for the run from its original corner to the new wall. Then mitre the new skirting and join it to the old.

If you cannot make a perfect match, the most practical, inexpensive and pleasing solution is not to make a match at all. Reproducing the pattern of moulded skirting is costly, and new skirting that fails to match the old exactly is generally obtrusive. Use instead a plain new skirting or clear pine board cut to the same height as the old skirting. The new skirting in this application butts against the old walls. With the mitre box at a 90-degree angle, square-cut the ends of the new skirting to fit their run, and nail them to the new wall. Then, using the same setting, cut the old skirting to lengths equal to the distance from their original corners to the face of the new skirting. Nail them into place *(right)*.

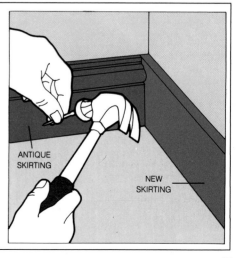

ANTIQUE SKIRTING

NEW SKIRTING

Removing Walls: Simpler Than You Think

Removing all or part of a wall, even one that is essential to the structure of the house, is a job within the capabilities of most homeowners. Before you start, make sure you understand all the wall's functions—besides serving as a partition, it may carry pipes or wiring—and know how well they can be served when it is gone.

Planning permission is not normally required to remove an interior wall, although you should submit your plans for building regulations approval before starting work, and be sure to seek professional advice if you suspect any complications.

To size up the job, look the wall over. The number of outlets and switches will indicate how much wiring lies inside it. A bathroom directly above may be hooked to plumbing that goes down through the wall.

If all you find is wiring that terminates at outlets in the wall, you can remove it when you break the wall. Even if you find many pipes and cables, you may be able to remove the bulk of the partition and leave part of one end of the wall to carry the various installations, which can be moved there by a plumber or an electrician.

More critically, you should be aware that the wall may bear weight from above, making it a vital structural element. If it does, you will have to limit the width of the opening to leave adequate support on either side of the hole; you will also have to support the weight above the wall while removing it, using adjustable props and needles *(page 59)*. To replace the load-bearing function of the wall, install a beam or lintel *(page 102)*, making an arch rather than removing the wall completely.

Load-bearing walls are usually made of brick or block, but you will occasionally find a timber stud load-bearing partition.

The clue to a load-bearing wall is joists crossing it at right angles *(below)*. You may be able to see the direction of the joists from your attic; you may have to cut a hole in the ceiling next to the wall to be removed. The area under the floorboards can also yield clues. If you find a girder or a wall running under and parallel to the partition in question, you can be quite sure that the partition carries weight down to this support. If any doubt remains, assume that the wall bears weight.

Unlike a load-bearing wall, a non-load-bearing wall usually runs parallel to the joists and perpendicular to the long walls of the house. Such walls do not bear any of the load of the house but are often an important part of the overall structure, acting in counterbalance to other walls at right angles to them, so check with an expert before attempting to remove them.

Load-bearing and non-loadbearing walls. This diagram shows how the total load of a house is passed down to its foundations. The roof is supported by outer walls (1) running parallel to the ridge and, through the triangular structure formed by the roof purlins, struts and binder, to the main interior load-bearing wall (2).

On upper floors, wooden joists running underneath the floorboards, at right angles to them, distribute the load of each room between the interior and exterior load-bearing walls. Sometimes an interior wall carries no roof load, only the load of upstairs rooms (3).

On the ground floor, the joists supporting the rooms rest on sleeper walls which carry the load directly to the foundations.

Non-loadbearing partition walls (4 and 5), which can be of brick, block or studwork, run either parallel or at right angles to the joists which carry their weight either to the load-bearing walls or directly to the foundations. Non-loadbearing walls are not continuous between floors so check under the floorboards to see if a wall is resting on the joists.

Some partitions may provide support to the structure of the house without bearing weight. The block partition shown here can be only partially removed as it provides an intermediate tie between two widely spaced load-bearing walls. The timber stud partition (5) serves no structural function and can be removed completely.

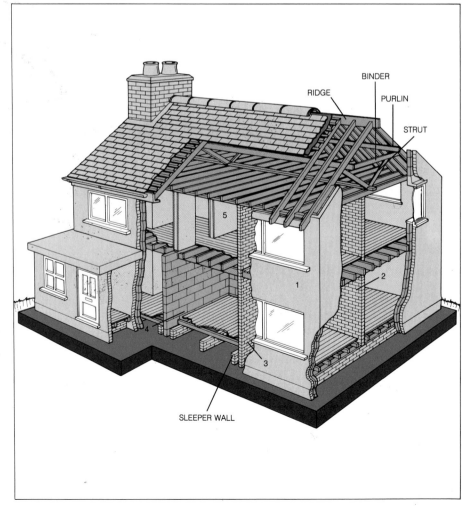

BINDER

RIDGE

PURLIN

STRUT

SLEEPER WALL

Taking Out a Non-Loadbearing Partition Wall

Once you have made sure that the wall you want to remove is not load-bearing, taking it out is a straightforward operation.

Before starting work, make sure that any plumbing and wiring installations in the wall are disconnected from the mains supply and decide where you are going to relocate them. Consult an electrician or plumber if you are in any doubt.

Removing a timber stud partition is the reverse of putting one in—first remove the skirting board, then the plasterboard, and finally cut away the studs and sole plate. Tearing off the surfaces of the wall you are removing is not difficult, but prepare for dirty work, especially if the material is plaster. When the wall is gone, you will be confronted by breaks in the ceiling, walls and floor. Ceilings and walls are easy to patch. The break in the floor of newly joined rooms can be built up with any wood as thick as the flooring, and the whole room can then be carpeted or tiled. If the floors are of parquet, and will remain exposed, you may need professional help to patch and refinish them.

1 Stripping the wall. Remove any skirting board or ceiling mouldings. Tape down dust sheets, close doors and open windows. Cut out the wall surfaces with a trimming knife, starting in a corner; once you have made a hole, the rest of the plasterboard can be stripped from both sides of the studs by hand. Saw the studs in two near the middle, and work the halves free from their nailing.

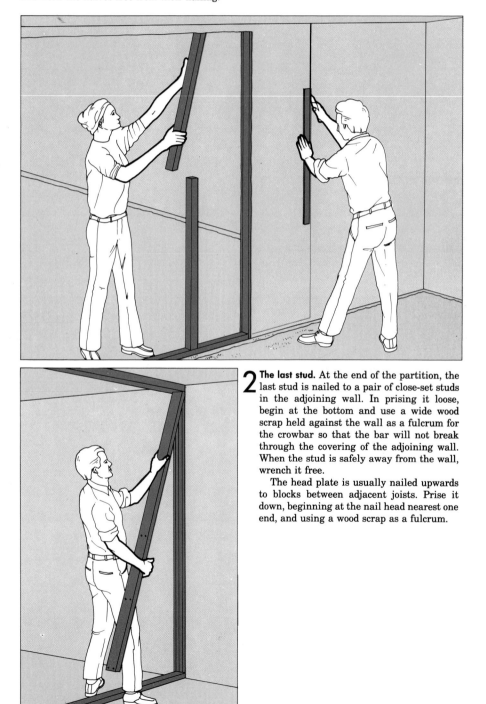

2 The last stud. At the end of the partition, the last stud is nailed to a pair of close-set studs in the adjoining wall. In prising it loose, begin at the bottom and use a wide wood scrap held against the wall as a fulcrum for the crowbar so that the bar will not break through the covering of the adjoining wall. When the stud is safely away from the wall, wrench it free.

The head plate is usually nailed upwards to blocks between adjacent joists. Prise it down, beginning at the nail head nearest one end, and using a wood scrap as a fulcrum.

3 **The sole plate.** Somewhere near the centre of the sole plate, make two saw cuts about 50 mm apart. Chisel out the wood between the cuts down to the subfloor. Insert a crowbar and lever up one end of the plate. With a scrap of timber as a fulcrum, lever up the other end.

Repair the gaps made in the adjoining walls and the ceiling as described on page 45. If you plan to cover the floor with resilient tiles or carpet, fill in the space where the sole plate rested with a board thick enough to even the surface.

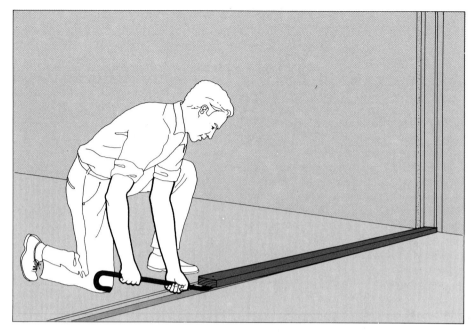

Leaving a Section in Place

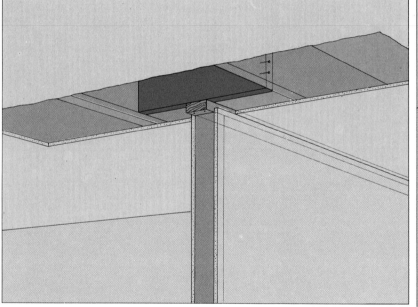

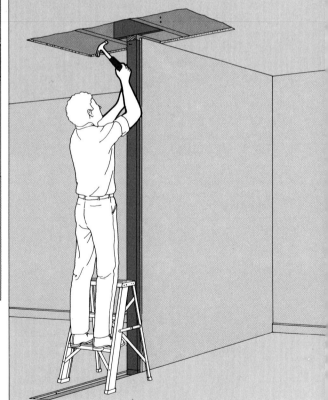

1 **Securing the head plate.** Remove the surface and studs *(page 57)* but not the head and sole plates of the wall, back to the stud nearest the end of the part you wish to preserve. Cut a hole about 300 mm wide in the ceiling, centred on the upper end of the stud and running to the second joist on either side. Saw the head plate off 50 mm out from the stud, and lever down the part of it remaining over the opening. Butt-nail a block as wide as the joists between the joists on each side of the head plate, resting the edge of the block on the outer end of the plate. Nail through the head plate up into the block.

2 **Reinforcing the stud.** Saw the sole plate down to floor level 50 mm out from the stud and chisel through the rest of it. Remove it as in Step 3, above. Nail a reinforcing stud, running from plate to plate, against the existing stud.

Patch the ceiling *(page 45)*; surface the reinforcing stud with plasterboard and finish it with tape and metal angle bead, using the techniques described on pages 46–47.

Making an Opening in a Load-Bearing Wall

Removing part of a load-bearing wall to make two rooms into one is a daunting task for an amateur builder, but the techniques used are not difficult to master. Check your local building regulations thoroughly before starting any work, and it is wise to seek professional advice to ensure that there are no complications relating to the structure of your home.

Load-bearing walls, which can be made of masonry or timber, carry the load of the rooms above—the floors, walls and roof, and anything in them. This load is transferred to the foundations of the house as shown on page 56. Before any part of the wall is removed, its load-bearing function must be redistributed to the remaining structure. This is done using a lintel—a rigid beam which is supported on sound

bearings at each end to take the weight above *(pages 102–103)*. Here, the bearings are piers of masonry left in place at each end of the opening, supporting a pre-stressed concrete lintel. If the wall is to be removed completely, the beam, usually a rolled steel joist (RSJ), must be firmly bedded into the walls on either side of the room. This is a complicated job, and is best done with the aid of a professional.

Before starting to make an opening in a load-bearing wall, you must support the weight above to prevent any movement in the structure damaging the rest of the building. This is done using adjustable steel props and timber bearers. Props can be hired from a builders' supplier: you will require a minimum of four pairs, two to support the ceiling above and two to hold

needles pushed through the wall above the lintel. Props should be positioned no more than 900 mm apart, so more pairs will be needed for a wider opening. The needles should be of sound, knot-free structural-grade timber, 75 or 100 mm square, and they should be long enough to give a clearance of up to 600 mm on either side of the wall you are knocking a hole in.

When all the brickwork has been removed, the opening is trimmed and then finished with metal angle bead which provides solid corners and a straight edge to plaster to. The floor is finished by filling in the gap with concrete, or by inserting timber bearers and floorboards. If the floors on each side of the opening are on different levels, make a step, or a sloping ramp between the rooms.

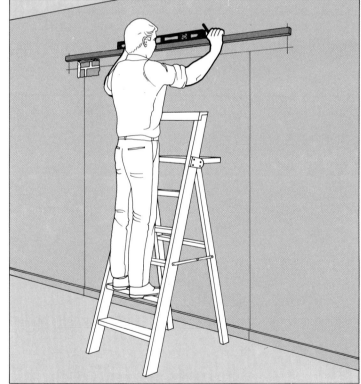

1 Positioning the opening and lintel. Outline the proposed opening, using a straightedge and level to ensure the lines are square and straight. Starting 15 mm above one of the corners, chisel away a small area of plaster to determine the position of the nearest brick or block course. Draw in the dimensions of the lintel, making sure that it will correspond with the brick courses at top and bottom and that there is an overhang of at least 150 mm on each side of the proposed opening. Remove skirting from both sides of the wall.

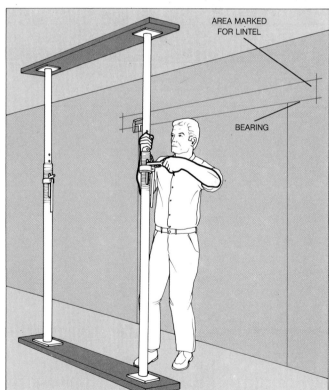

2 Supporting the ceiling. If the joists in the ceiling above run at right angles to the wall, position adjustable props a maximum of 600 mm out from the wall on either side, no more than 900 mm apart. Support the ceiling joists with a scaffold board running at right angles to the joists, and resting on the props. Stand the props on scaffold board to distribute the load evenly and protect the floor beneath. If you are working on a first or second-floor room, prop the floors beneath in exactly the same way.

3 **Making holes for the needles.** About 150 mm in from either end of the proposed opening, draw lines vertically upwards using a straightedge. About two brick courses above the lintel, between the two lines, mark the positions for the needles. Remove the plaster from the marked areas and, using a jointing chisel, bolster and lump hammer, carefully take out enough masonry to make holes big enough for the needles. Clean all the mortar off the bricks above the holes, so that the needles, when in place, will bear on masonry not mortar.

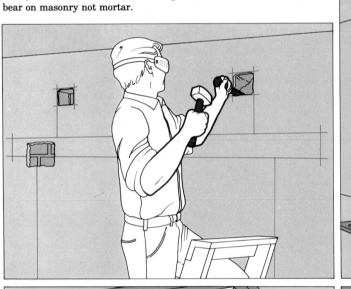

4 **Supporting the needles.** Slide the needles through the wall, supporting both ends with adjustable props placed on scaffold boards no more than 600 mm from the wall. Use a level to check the props are vertical and the needles are level. Adjust the props gradually in turn until the needles are firmly butted up against the tops of the holes, providing a rigid support for the wall above. Nail the end plates of the props to the boards.

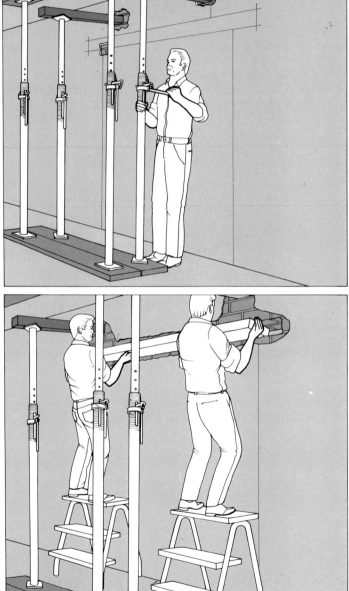

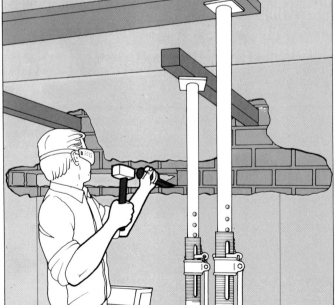

5 **Making the hole for the lintel.** Chisel off the plaster in the area marked for the lintel, plus 25 mm all round. Using a hammer and bolster, remove the whole brick course, working from both sides of the wall if necessary, and taking care not to dislodge the mortar holding the course above. Clean out all the mortar from the top of the course below, to give a level seat for the lintel.

6 **Installing the lintel.** With a helper, carefully lift the lintel, making sure that it is the correct way up, and slide it into position in the centre of the hole. The lintel should finish flush with the brickwork, leaving approximately 15 mm on either side to be filled with plaster at a later stage.

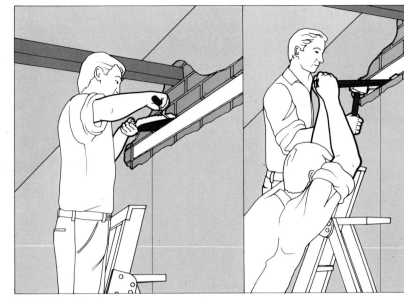

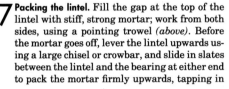

7 Packing the lintel. Fill the gap at the top of the lintel with stiff, strong mortar; work from both sides, using a pointing trowel *(above)*. Before the mortar goes off, lever the lintel upwards using a large chisel or crowbar, and slide in slates between the lintel and the bearing at either end to pack the mortar firmly upwards, tapping in extra slates until the lintel is firmly pressed against the underside of the wall above *(above)*. Check the lintel is level from both sides, adjusting with more slates if necessary. Extend the lines marking the outer edges of the opening up on to the lintel. Leave the lintel to settle for two days before knocking down the wall.

8 Knocking through the opening. Remove all the plaster inside the marked area with a bolster. Starting in the centre, remove the first course beneath the lintel, using a lump hammer and bolster or a heavy-duty electric hammer with a chisel attachment. Knock down the rest of the opening course by course up to the marks; take care not to dislodge mortar beyond the opening.

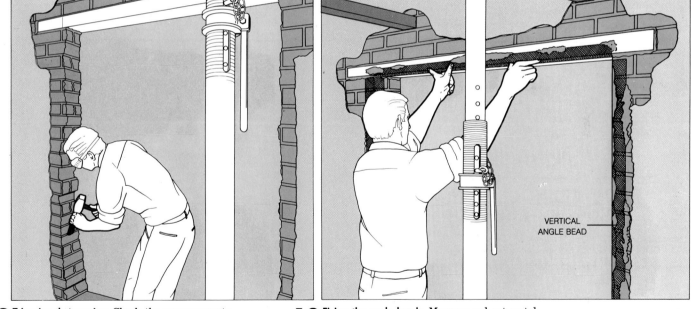

VERTICAL ANGLE BEAD

9 Trimming the opening. Check the measurements of the opening again, using a level from the marks on the lintel, and trim off the ends of any protruding bricks. Measure and mark about 100 mm back from the edge of the opening and round the needles. Trim off all the plaster within this area ready to fix the angle beads.

10 Fixing the angle beads. Measure and cut metal angle bead to fit the edges on both sides, using a hacksaw. Trowel mixed finishing plaster on to the inside of each vertical bead at 300 mm intervals, offer it up to the wall, pressing it firmly against the corner, and check that it is straight and vertical over its whole length, using a straightedge and level. Check the width of the opening at the top, middle and bottom repeatedly, until the beads are completely parallel. Trim the top beads to fit inside the vertical beads, and fix them as before, checking carefully for level.

Finishing the Opening

1 **Taking down the supports.** When the angle beads are firmly set, unscrew the wall and ceiling props, and remove the needles from the wall. Fill both the needle holes, using whole bricks if possible, and mortar them carefully in place.

2 **Applying base coat.** Using a plasterer's float, apply a layer of base coat, made from sand, cement and lime in the proportion 5:1:1, to the exposed brickwork round the opening and over the needle holes, bringing it up to about 2 mm below the level of the existing plaster.

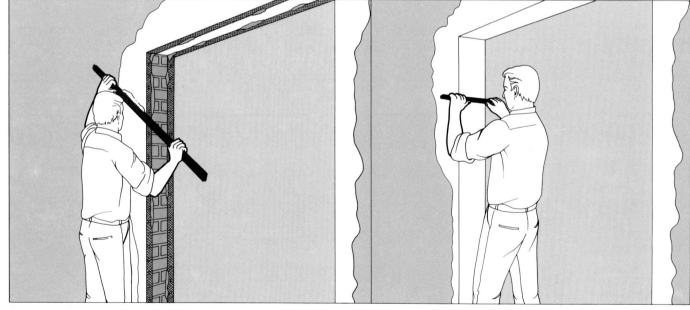

3 **Smoothing the base coat.** Use a straight piece of timber, approximately 1 metre long, as a levelling stick to strike off excess base coat; work from the floor upwards, and use a side-to-side sawing motion *(above, left)*. Move across the lintel with the levelling stick held at an angle of 45 degrees. Repeat the process for the reveals and underside of the lintel, striking off to the angle beads; use a shorter levelling stick for this *(above, right)*.

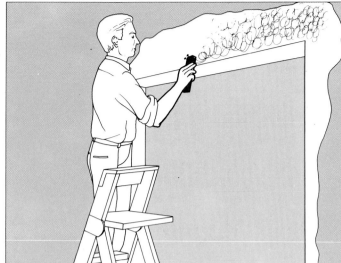

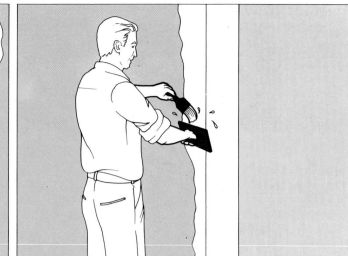

4 **Keying the base coat.** Leave the wall until the entire coat is touch-dry. Make a scratcher by driving two nails through a block of wood, so that their points protrude 2 mm. Use a circular action to score the surface of the base coat and provide a key for the finish plaster.

5 **Finishing the opening.** Cover the base coat with finish plaster, smoothing it with the trailing edge of the plasterer's float. Leave the plaster to set for about 20 minutes, then test to see if the surface is firm by pressing it gently with your thumb. Use a large clean paintbrush to wet the plaster with clean water, and float off the surface to give a good smooth finish.

Finishing the Floor

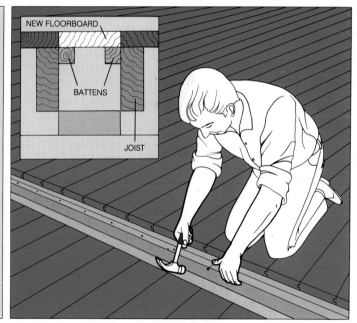

A concrete floor. If the floor on one or both sides of the opening is concrete, fill the space left by the removal of the wall with a stiff mix of ballast, sand and cement in the proportion of 3:2:1, tamping it down with a float or a piece of timber to compact the mix. Strike off excess concrete, and trowel the surface to give a smooth finish.

A timber floor. If the joists run parallel to the wall, nibble down the remaining brickwork below the existing floor level to give enough space to attach 37 by 37 mm battens inside the joists on either side of the opening flush with the top. Nail pieces of floorboard or chipboard floor panels to the battens to bridge the gap.

If the joists are at right angles to the wall, level the brickwork down to the bottom of the joists, then fit new sections of joist to bridge the gap, finishing with floorboards as before.

4

Solid Floors and Versatile Ceilings

A rich parquet flooring. An ideal covering for a timber or concrete floor, these varnished wooden parquet blocks are held in place with a viscous mastic adhesive. After the tiles are placed in the mastic, a wooden block and a mallet are used to tap them together; this will ensure a close fit and a smooth finish.

Creating any new living space usually involves installing or replacing a floor or a ceiling or both. Just patching the existing surface is usually less satisfactory in the long run than putting in a new one. For one thing, you will want the kind of overhead shelter and underfoot support that both suit your taste and match the uses you plan for your new room. And, in most cases, putting in a new floor or ceiling requires very little more work than extensively repairing an old one.

Ceilings and floors constructed with forethought and a moderate outlay of time and money can contribute much to comfort and appearance. In many cases they make up for architectural deficiencies. Dividing a room, for example, may make the ceiling too high for the room size; lowering the ceiling restores proper proportions. Recessing light fixtures can make a low ceiling seem higher. Soundproofing a ceiling or a floor can deaden noise from upstairs or downstairs and adapt a room for use as a study or a home office. By merely colouring or texturing a floor you can change the whole look and function of a room: a basement becomes a children's playroom with tough, bright-bordered tiles underfoot; an enclosed garage turns into a study with deep-toned parquet under a small rug; an attic is transformed into a bedroom where cool-coloured tiles catch and amplify the light from roof windows.

Planning and preparation, essential to any home improvement project, are especially important in the case of floors and ceilings. Floors, particularly, demand solid foundations since they take more of a beating than any other surface in the house. A well-built floor, such as the one on pages 66–73, is much more than a surface; it is a many-layered structure starting, perhaps, from a concrete slab that must be levelled and waterproofed, and continuing with wooden joists or sleepers, subflooring, underlayment and finally a finish that can be anything from elegant parquet to colourful plastic.

Support for a ceiling is less complicated. Most ceilings are simply attached directly to the joists that support the floor of the room above, or to battens nailed at intervals across a concrete ceiling *(pages 74–76)*. Where no ceiling joists exist, as in an attic, you can nail new joists across rafters *(pages 98–99)* and attach the ceiling to them. Hanging a suspended ceiling *(pages 79–81)* requires little more technical skill than hanging a picture; prefabricated snap-together metal strips strung from the ceiling provide a framework for drop-in panels.

Devising a pattern of tiles or panels to cover a floor or ceiling tidily and symmetrically can be a fascinating geometrical exercise. By using the techniques on page 72 you can even fit floor tiles round corners and such irregularities as thresholds and doorjambs with professional ease.

A Base for a Floor: Level, Smooth, Waterproof

If you decide that a new floor is needed in the extra living space you have created, cemented-down tiles—available in a wide variety of materials *(pages 70–73)*—are the simplest to use.

Since cemented-down tiles show every lump, bump and nail head beneath them, or buckle unless they are seated properly, these tiles must be laid over a carefully prepared and perfectly smooth surface. The concrete slab of a basement or garage will serve as the floor for a room for occasional use if it is first levelled and waterproofed *(below and opposite page, above)*. However, a better finish can be achieved on a concrete slab if you install a composite floor, in which wooden sleepers are laid on the concrete slab and then covered with chipboard panels and a layer of hardboard underlayment *(pages 68–69)*. The tiles, when laid, are then much less likely to peel off, and the wooden platform adds spring to make the result much more comfortable to walk on than tiles that are in direct contact with the concrete slab. If you wish to insulate a floor against noise and heat loss, lay a chipboard subfloor over a layer of insulation material.

In an attic, a subfloor will have to be laid over joists *(pages 90–91)* in order to provide a base for a finish floor.

Regardless of the type of floor that is to be installed over concrete, the slab itself should be moistureproofed first. A bitumastic waterproofing compound, which is readily available at most builders' merchants and is applied like paint with a paintbrush, will do the trick if your basement feels dry, and if you are planning to tile or paint directly over it. For a raised floor, cover the concrete slab with polythene sheeting before putting down the timber sleepers *(opposite page, centre)*. Neither treatment, of course, will protect your flooring if you are plagued by water in your basement; such a serious problem should be solved, by a professional if necessary, before any flooring is laid.

Preparing a Concrete Slab

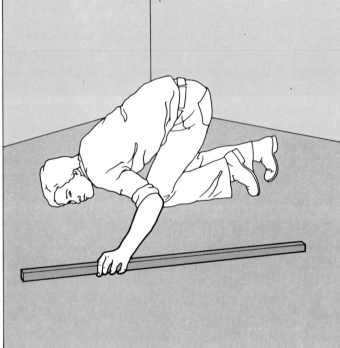

1 **Smoothing the surface.** Move a long straightedge over the floor surface, bending down to check for gaps underneath. Fill any indentation more than 6 mm deep with cement mortar, applied over a coating of PVA bonding agent to improve adhesion. Flatten bumps more than 6 mm with an abrasive stone. Sweep the floor, and then clean it thoroughly with a strong sugar soap solution, to remove any dirt and grease.

2 **Waterproofing the slab.** Working from the corner of the room farthest from the door, prime the floor with a coating of bitumastic waterproofing compound diluted with water, according to the manufacturer's instructions. When the surface is dry, brush on one or two undiluted coatings.

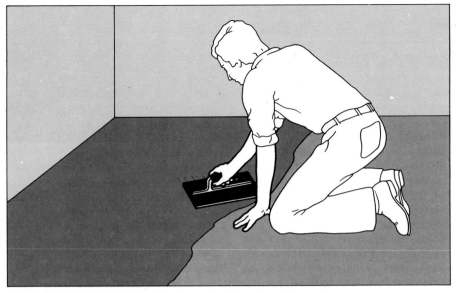

3 **Levelling the slab.** Set a spirit level on a long straightedge, and move it over the floor to see if the floor is level. Mix self-levelling latex cement smoothing compound to a creamy consistency, following the manufacturer's instructions. Beginning in a corner of the room, pour the mixture on to the floor, a little at a time. Smooth each patch with a steel float, to form an even layer about 4 mm thick. Cover the entire floor in this way, then leave it to smooth out and set. Check the surface is level with the spirit level and straightedge and apply a second coat if necessary.

Supports for a Subfloor

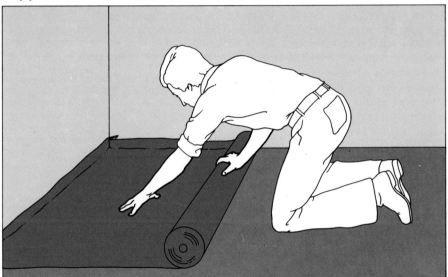

1 **Laying polythene sheeting.** When a concrete slab is used as the base for timber sleepers, subfloor underlayment and finish flooring, it need not be level but it must be dry. A layer of 250 micron (1000-gauge) polythene or polythene-bitumen provides an effective barrier against moisture. Unroll the sheeting, smoothing it flat as you go, and tuck it neatly into the angle between floor and wall, leaving a 75 mm flap all round to extend up the wall face.

2 **Sleepers for a slab.** To provide a base for a floor on a concrete slab, lay lengths of 100 by 50 mm pre-treated timber across the room at 400 mm intervals, measured from centre to centre. Do not screw the sleepers to the floor; the subfloor will hold them in place.

Subfloor and Underlayment

A subfloor should provide a sound, noise-free platform on which to lay finish flooring. Unless you are installing a floating floor *(page 91)*, you will find it easier to fit a subfloor before any new walls are put up, mainly because the subfloor, once it is fitted, will give you something to stand on while building the walls. Add the underlayment and finish flooring after the walls are in place.

Chipboard is an excellent subfloor material. The tongue and groove sheets—18 or 22 mm thick and 2440 by 1220 mm or 610 mm—are larger than wooden floorboards, and therefore easier to install; and because the floor has fewer joints it is virtually squeakproof if properly installed.

To obtain maximum strength from a chipboard subfloor, lay the sheets in a staggered pattern with their longer edges at right angles to the wooden sleeper joists. Because the tongue and groove joints are rigid, they do not need additional support, and therefore do not have to lie directly over the sleepers.

Finish flooring, whether it consists of vinyl, parquet or cork tiles, must be laid on a perfectly smooth surface. An underlayment *(opposite page, above)* will smooth over any minor unevenness in the subfloor, and will also prevent damage to the finish floor from nails forced upwards by movement of joists as they settle, expand or contract. New underlayment should also be laid when installing a new finish floor on old floorboards, to give an even surface.

In kitchens, bathrooms and other areas that may be wet, use specially treated, moisture-resistant chipboard for the subfloor and oil-tempered hardboard for the underlayment. Elsewhere, use 1220 by 1220 mm squares of untempered hardboard, very smooth on one side but rough on the other, to hold the finish flooring adhesive. Just before installation, unpack the hardboard sheets and dampen them, so that the sheets contract on drying after they are installed; this means they will not subsequently buckle and damage the finish floor. The rows of underlayment are laid across those of the subfloor at right angles. If you use nails, screws or staples instead of adhesive *(box, opposite)* to fasten the underlayment to the subfloor, be sure the fasteners do not penetrate the wooden sleeper joists. Otherwise, like the subfloor nails, they may be forced upwards by joist movement and mar the finish flooring.

Installing the subfloor. Before starting to cut and lay the subfloor panels, work out a pattern that avoids alignment of joints, while requiring a minimum of chipboard. Use untrimmed full sheets as far as possible. Begin by marking the wall above the centre of each row of sleeper joists at both sides of the room. As you lay the panels, use a straightedge and a pencil to extend the sleeper lines across the panels as a nailing guide.

Fasten the chipboard to the sleepers with 37 mm lost-head nails spaced at 200 mm intervals, setting the nails 25 mm in from the edges of the chipboard panels.

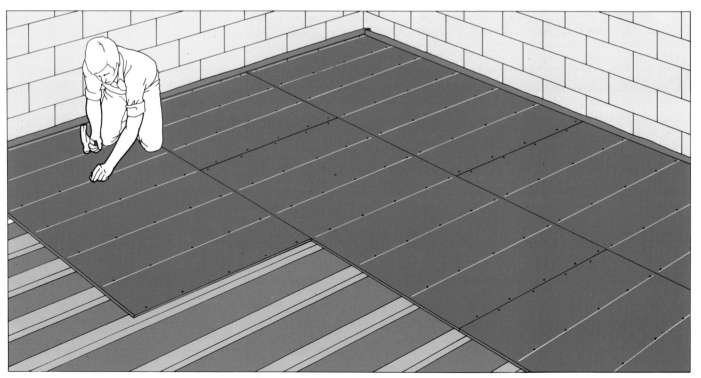

Installing the underlayment. Hardboard underlayment *(dark lines in the drawing below)* must be laid so that it always spans the subfloor joints *(light lines)* and, like the subfloor, it must be arranged in a staggered pattern. If you lay the subfloor before erecting walls and install the underlayment afterwards, this overlapping is almost automatic, since the underlayment sheets will be offset from the subfloor by the thickness of the walls. Place the underlayment sheets—rough surface up—3 mm in from the walls; separate the sheets from each other by less than 1 mm, roughly the thickness of thin card. To fit the last sheet in each row, follow the procedure used for border tiles, as demonstrated on page 72. Unless underlayment sheets are to be stuck down with adhesive *(box, below)*, fasteners should be spaced 100 mm apart over the entire sheet and 9 mm in from the edges. You may find it helpful to mark off the surface of each sheet in 100 mm squares as a guide.

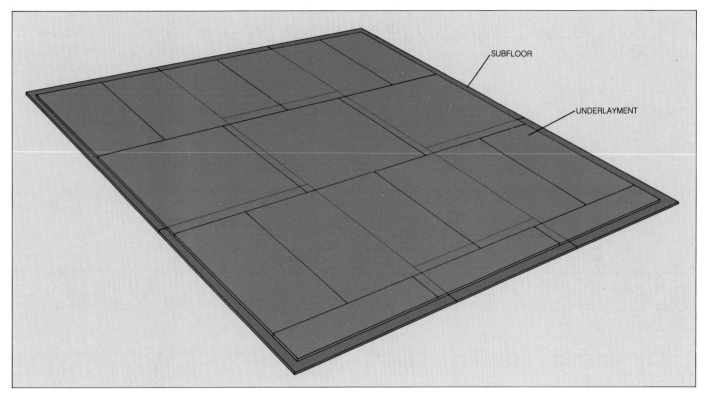

SUBFLOOR

UNDERLAYMENT

Four Fastening Methods

Underlayment can be attached to the subfloor in a variety of ways. They all work, but some work better—or save more time—than others.

☐ LOST-HEAD NAILS (25 mm long) are well suited to the task, and have thin heads that will sink flush with the surface (ordinary headed nails would create lumps that might show through resilient tile). You can also use special 12 to 25 mm hardboard nails, known as deep-drive or diamond-point pins. These nails have a thin, pointed head which disappears into the wood when the nails are fully hammered in.

☐ SCREWS can be sunk flush with the surface of the underlayment and will always remain in place. However, this method of fastening is extremely time consuming, given the number of screws and screwholes needed for just one sheet.

☐ STAPLES are used by most professional builders. This technique is fast and, if done correctly, leaves no tell-tale lumps on the underlayment surface. The 12 to 18 mm heavy-duty staples required for the job are driven by a spring-loaded staple gun. Practise with some waste board before you start, since it is easy to drive staples either too far into the surface, or not far enough, or sideways.

☐ ADHESIVE, applied to the subfloor, is used by many contractors to affix underlayment. Use a proprietary contact adhesive in a well-ventilated room. You should plan the position of the sheets carefully beforehand, because the adhesive cannot be separated once contact has taken place. If the underlayment is hardboard, roughen the downward facing surface with coarse sandpaper to create the texture needed for firm sticking.

Laying Tiles to Finish the Floor

Tiles make a serviceable and handsome flooring for any remodelled room. They can be made of ceramic, cork, asphalt, wood or vinyl. All types of tile are set down in much the same way, although there may be some minor differences cementing them in place and cutting them for borders. On these pages and overleaf, the basic tile-laying process is described as it applies to vinyl or cork, the two most popular tile materials. With only slight variations, the same system serves for another popular tile—wood block (*page 73*).

No matter what the material, write down the dimensions of your room so that you can calculate the number of tiles you will require. Most wood or cork tiles are 225 mm square; divide the length and width of your room (in mm) by 225, and multiply the two results. Add 10 per cent to allow for wastage. The final figure will give you the number of tiles you require.

Vinyl, cork and wood block tiles are all available in self-sticking versions, with adhesive on the underside of the tile beneath backing paper. However, this layer of glue is thin, and you can achieve a much better bond by using dry tiles that are laid in adhesive applied to the flooring material, whether the flooring material consists of hardboard panels or concrete screed. Ask your dealer for the correct adhesive.

Tiles should be laid in a pyramid pattern over half the floor at a time; this method helps ensure straight rows and snug fits, since you will always have guidance on two sides when putting the tiles in place. The starting point for most tile pyramids is set with the aid of a chalk line to avoid having to cut narrow strips for borders; for some tiles the starting point is the centre of areas subject to heavy traffic, such as doorways (*page 73, Step 1*).

If you are laying adhesive-backed tiles on hardboard underlayment, brush wood sealer over the hardboard and allow it to dry; the sealer will keep the tiles' thin layer of glue from being soaked up by the absorbent hardboard. If you use dry tiles, cover half the room with adhesive, starting at one wall; then lay tiles from the centre of the room, crouching or kneeling on those already in place. Repeat the process for the other half of the room.

A Dry Run to Find the Starting Point

1 Lining up the tiles. Chalk a length of string and tie it tautly between two nails set in the exact middle of opposite walls of the room. Without snapping the string, place a tile at the approximate centre of the line, its edge on the string bisecting the room. From this starting point lay a row of dry tiles to the wall, perpendicular to the line. If the last tile in the row leaves a space of 50 mm or more to the wall, proceed to Step 2. If there is less than a 50 mm space, move the row so the last tile is up against the wall. This ensures that tiles will be even at borders.

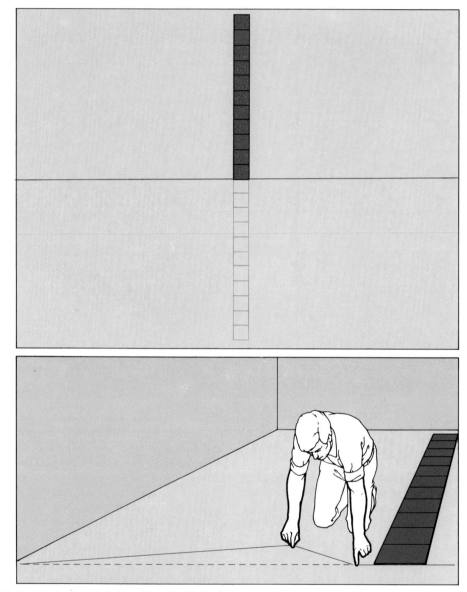

2 Marking the first chalk line. Align the chalked string so that it runs along the edge of the first tile in the row, moving the string if necessary. Press down on the chalked string in the middle of the room. Snap one side of the string and then the other so that a chalk line is deposited.

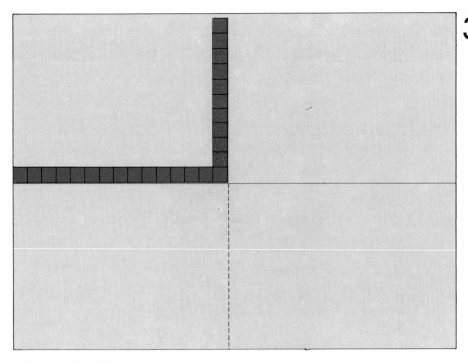

3 **Marking the second line.** Place a second row of tiles at right angles to the first, with the row's edge on the chalk line *(solid line)*. If the last tile in the new row leaves a space of less than 50 mm to the wall, slide both the new row and the first row towards that wall until the last tile is up against the wall. Snap another chalk line *(dotted line)* along the edge of the first row of tiles. Then remove all the tiles.

Placing the Tiles

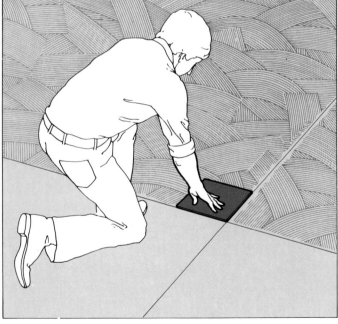

1 **Starting the pyramid.** If you are using adhesive-backed tiles, strip off the backing paper from the undersides and lay the tiles directly on the underlayment, beginning at the right angle formed by the intersection of the two chalk lines in the middle of the room.

For dry tiles, first spread adhesive over half the room at a time with a notched trowel, starting at the walls and working back down to the centre of the room. Take care not to cover the chalk lines. As with adhesive-backed tiles, begin laying the tiles at the chalk line intersection.

2 **The emplacement technique.** As you lay tiles in a pyramid pattern *(inset)*, butt each new tile against an edge of one already laid and drop the new tile in place; sliding it into position would force adhesive up and on to the tile's surface.

Custom Cuts for Borders

Cutting tiles for borders. Place a tile squarely over the fixed tile closest to the border. Hold a second tile over it up against the wall. Using the second tile's edge as a guide, score the first tile with a trimming knife. Snap the scored tile. One piece will just fit into the border area.

Cutting tiles for corners. Place a tile squarely over the last fixed tile on the left side of the corner. Hold a second tile over the first up against the border. Using the second tile's edge as a guide, mark the first with a pencil *(below)*. Next move the first tile, without turning it, to a position squarely over the fixed tile closest to the right side of the border. Again using an overlying tile as your guide, make a second pencil line *(below, right)*. Cut the marked tile along the pencil lines and fit it into the corner.

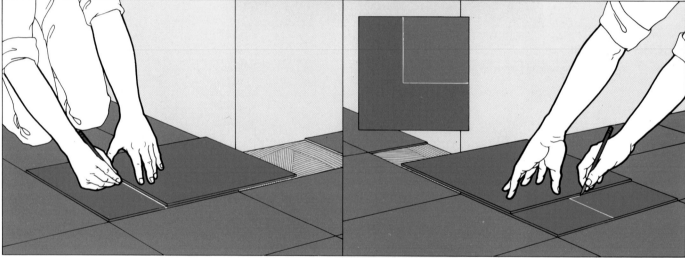

Fitting tiles to irregular areas. This is done in much the same way as shaping tiles for borders. Move the top tile along the irregular length of wall—in this case an ornate architrave—so that the appropriate corner fits successive surfaces. With each change of position, mark the underlying tile. Here, for example, the marks in the drawings on the right correspond to similarly designated portions of the architrave. If there is a curved area, bend a piece of wire—wire solder is ideal if you have some in your workshop—to transfer the curve to the tile being fitted, as on the far right. Connect the various marks, cut through the tile with a trimming knife, and then fit the tile into position.

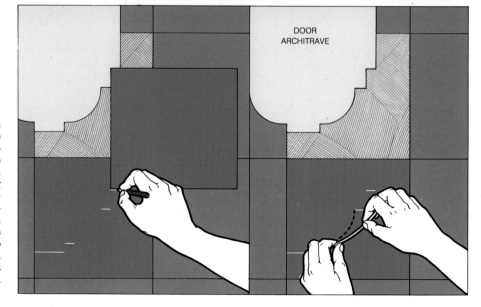

Shortcut to a Hardwood Floor

Wood block or parquet flooring provides a hardwood finish without requiring the finicky work of nailing, sanding and sealing which is involved with wood boards. The square blocks, made of glued layers or strips of prefinished teak or other hardwood, come in many sizes and patterns.

Like vinyl tiles, wood block is available in both dry and self-sticking versions, and is installed using the same basic methods, with a few variations. For one thing whole blocks are placed in doorways or in other heavy traffic areas; this is necessary because the glue will stand up best under constant stress if it is under a full-sized block. The glue itself is different from that used on other tiles: wood blocks require mastic, which is a more viscous substance than standard tile adhesive. Some blocks have an interlocking tongue and groove feature to help hold them in place.

Wood blocks also absorb moisture; let them stand loosely for a week in the room where they will be laid, to adjust to humidity levels, or they may buckle or shrink after installation. A cork expansion strip, fitted between the wall and the edge of the tiled floor, will ensure that minor changes after the floor is laid do not cause damage.

If the room next to the newly finished wood block floor has carpet that projects into the threshold between rooms, fold the carpet under itself until it is flush with the wood block and tack it down with carpet tacks. However, if the carpet does not project into the threshold, or if the adjacent room is covered with wood strip or resilient tiles, a metal carpet gripper must be used to ensure a smooth—and safe—joint.

1 Marking the chalk lines. Begin a row of loose blocks in the centre of a doorway with the first block set completely through the threshold *(inset)*. Lay tiles to the middle of the room. If there is no other door, mark a chalk line at right angles to the row, using the edge of the last block as your guide; then lay a second row along that line and snap a chalk line at right angles to the first one (that is, alongside the first row).

If there is another doorway in an adjoining wall *(below)*, lay the second row of blocks from the centre of, and through, the threshold to the middle of the room. Shift both rows so the last block in one row aligns with the last block in the other. Snap the second chalk line along the side of the first row. Remove the blocks.

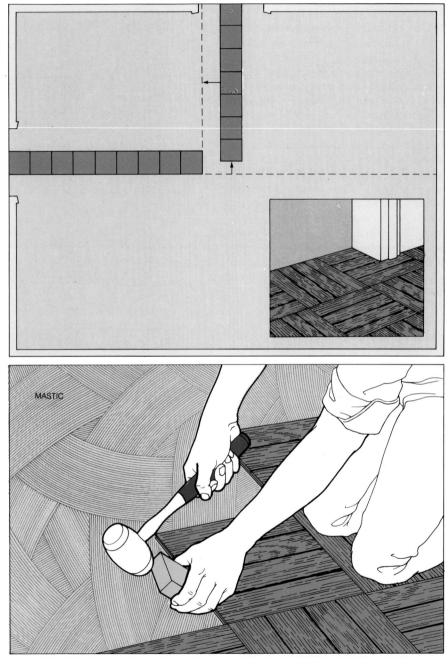

MASTIC

2 Laying the blocks. Spread a layer of mastic 3 mm thick over half the room, using a notched trowel. Lay wood blocks in a pyramid pattern, as described in Step 2 on page 71. Press the squares together, then place a block of wood at each edge and tap it gently with a mallet to ensure a tight fit. An extra square of parquet is ideal for this; however, if you are using tongue and groove blocks, remember to fit tongue against tongue and groove against groove before using the mallet.

Cut blocks at borders and round doorways using the techniques described opposite, but allowing a 12 mm gap between the last tile and the wall. Fit a cork expansion strip (usually supplied with the tiles) to fill the gap.

Techniques for Finishing a Ceiling

When a ceiling is added to a new living space most people finish it with tiles, acoustic panels or plasterboard sheets. Plasterboard is the most adaptable finish, but tiles or acoustic panels are simpler to install in some cases, and their sound-absorbing qualities are often very useful. Both tiles and panels are easily marred—a fact to consider in planning the ceiling of a playroom or any low-beamed room—and repainting them is more difficult than refinishing plasterboard. Tiles can be installed on an unfinished ceiling (or on one in poor condition) by gluing *(page 77)*. An alternative method is to suspend a grid of metal strips and place acoustic or plasterboard panels in them. A suspended ceiling *(pages 79–81)* may be best if you wish to lower the ceiling, or if you need to cover pipes and ducts extending below the joists. A suspended ceiling with removable panels also allows great flexibility in installing overhead lights and permits access to hidden fixtures such as shut-off valves in water supply pipes. You can buy complete suspended ceiling packages that include both panels and metal supports, designed to suit your own particular needs.

When fixing plasterboard directly to a ceiling, make a plan of the ceiling before you start, and decide on the position of the sheets *(Step 3)*. For a timber ceiling, install sheets at right angles to the joists, bearing in mind that the ends of the sheets must land on the centre lines of joists, and that joints must be staggered to prevent a continuous seam on a single joist. For a concrete ceiling, fit wooden battens first to provide nailing surfaces. Try to arrange the panels so that cut edges lie next to the wall, and that joints consist of two bevelled edges together wherever possible to enable you to make a smooth finish with jointing compound and tape *(pages 46–47)*.

For a sloping ceiling under a staircase or in an attic *(pages 98–99)*, hold the plasterboard sheets with supporting nails while fixing them in position *(page 76)*. You may find it easier to work with smaller panels called plaster lath, which are manufactured especially for use in confined spaces and fitted in the same way.

Preparing a concrete ceiling for plasterboard. Cut 50 by 25 mm wooden battens to go round the edges of the ceiling, and secure them with 63 mm No. 8 screws and plugs. Check they lie flat, shimming them from behind if necessary.

Referring to your ceiling plan, cut and fit bat- tens across the shortest dimension of the ceiling at 1200 mm intervals, then fit additional battens between them at 400 mm intervals, checking each one against the others with a straightedge and spirit level to make sure that the undersides are level and flat.

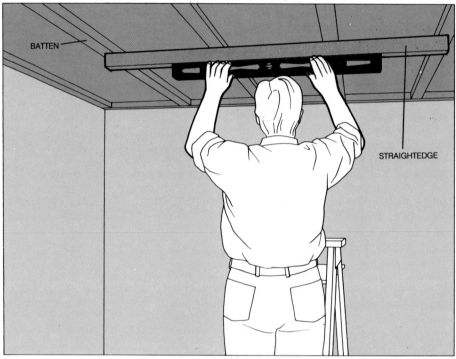

Fitting a Plasterboard Ceiling

1 **Marking guidelines for nails.** Make a vertical mark on the plates or wall below the centre of each joist or batten end. The marks will establish the sight lines your plasterboard nails must follow after the plasterboard sheets hide the joist or batten itself.

2 Putting up plasterboard. Start in a corner and butt the sheets in a continuous line, scribing them to fit *(page 9)* if the walls are uneven. Get someone to help you lift the plasterboard, which is too heavy for one person to handle. Make a T-brace the height of your ceiling for your assistant to use in holding up the sheet while you nail. When you have the end of a sheet centred on the joist or batten where it will join the next sheet, push the first nails into the board 12 mm from the edge at 400 mm intervals. Standard 30 mm plasterboard nails are made sharp enough to penetrate the board. To drive them home, try the position professional plasterboard hangers use. Hold the hammer in front of your face, with your thumb against the handle, and hit the nails by rotating your wrist and forearm *(inset)*.

3 Nailing and fitting. Fit the plasterboard according to your plan, making sure the ends of the sheets land on the centre lines of joists and that joints are staggered as in the plan here. Nail at 400 mm intervals along the joist or batten lines. Dimple the board round each nail as described on page 44, Step 2. To cut short or narrow pieces, score and break as shown on page 42. Measure holes for lighting or ventilation *(page 43)*, and cut holes for fittings before installing the board. Finish the joints between panels with jointing compound and tape *(pages 46–47)*. Similarly, fill the dimples with jointing compound.

POSITION OF LIGHT FITTING

JOIST

Under the Stairs: a Special Method for a Sloping Ceiling

1 **Supporting the sheets.** Measure the area to be covered, then cut the plasterboard; add 50 mm to the width for trimming. Cut a 50 by 25 mm wooden batten the length of the staircase and nail it to the back of each step, between the staircase stringers; shim if necessary to bring it up to the bottom edge of the stringers. Tack 75 mm nails part way into the wall, 25 mm below the inner staircase stringer, at 400 mm intervals.

2 **Nailing the plasterboard.** Slide the plasterboard behind the support nails and butt it up against the wall. Hold the other side of the sheet in place and, using plasterboard nails every 200 mm, fix the sheet to the stringers and batten, starting with the easiest position for you to reach.

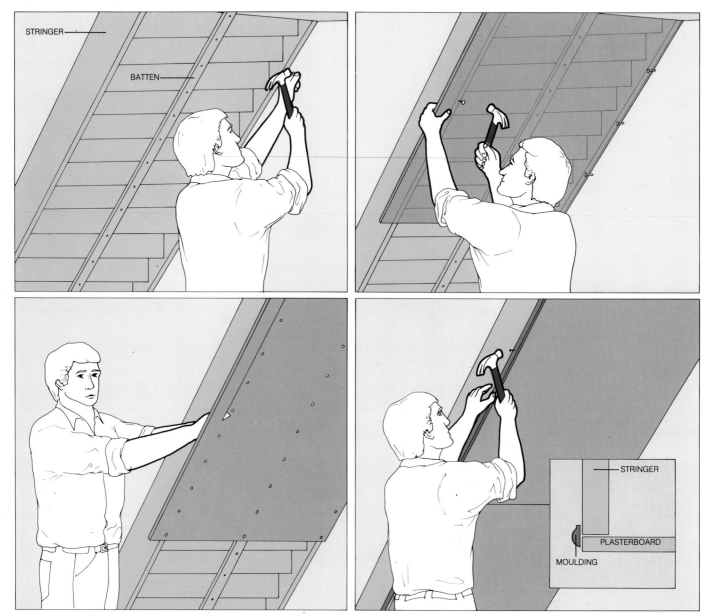

3 **Trimming the sheet.** Score carefully down the back of the plasterboard with a trimming knife, flush with the edge of the outer staircase stringer *(above)*. Snap the board downwards from the cut and slice through the front paper, trimming it to give a neat finish.

4 **Finishing the edges.** If the staircase stringer is to be left open, nail decorative moulding to cover the cut edge of the plasterboard *(above and inset)*. If the adjoining wall is of plaster or plasterboard, finish the exposed corner of the staircase with metal corner bead and jointing compound.

A Quick and Easy Method for a Tiled Ceiling

A tiled ceiling makes an attractive covering for damaged and uneven concrete, plaster or plasterboard, and provides a simple and inexpensive way to create a decorative ceiling for a new living space.

Standard-sized ceiling tiles are 300 mm square, with bevelled edges, and the majority can be fixed to the existing ceiling with adhesive. The most common type is made of 10 mm thick expanded polystyrene. You can increase heat insulation, reduce condensation, and obtain a more lasting finish by using tiles made of 19 mm-thick pressed wood fibre or vinyl-coated mineral fibre. These tiles are also available with tongued and grooved edges, which can be either stuck on, or tacked or stapled to ceiling battens (page 74). To reduce noise levels in a children's playroom or music room, use acoustic tiles, which are specially designed to absorb sound. Both mineral fibre and acoustic tiles can also be used with a suspended ceiling grid (pages 79–81) to reduce the height of a room.

To allow for any unevenness in the length of the walls when fixing tiles with adhesive, tile in rows across the room from a central point. Fix corner and edge tiles last of all, and measure and cut each one individually to ensure a neat fit.

Apply the adhesive to a clean, grease-free surface. Many adhesives will not stick to paint so, if the old ceiling was painted, strip it down, or go over the ceiling with a wire brush on a power drill to score the surface and provide a key for the adhesive. For a plasterboard ceiling, size the surface before tiling to stop the adhesive being absorbed into the plasterboard.

Decide on the position of your lighting fixtures, and have any rewiring done before you start to tile the ceiling. When relocating a ceiling rose, make sure it will be more or less in the middle of a tile, and switch off the electricity supply while you are tiling round the fitting. When tiling is complete, cover any gap between the edges of the wall and the ceiling using a moulding of plasterboard, polystyrene or timber, as shown on pages 54–55.

1 Planning the job. At ceiling level, make a chalk mark at the centre of each wall. Measure from each mark to an adjoining corner. Divide this distance by the size of your ceiling tiles—here, 300 mm square. If the amount left over is less than 150 mm, move the centre markers 150 mm right or left. Mark 300 mm intervals from the centre markers to the adjoining walls (below). To estimate the number of tiles you will require, count the number of 300 mm intervals on two adjoining walls; add one to each of these figures and multiply them. To provide a guideline for fixing the tiles, drive nails into the centre markers on one pair of facing walls, and snap a chalk line across the ceiling between them. Then do the same in the other direction. Start tiling where the two lines intersect in the centre of the ceiling.

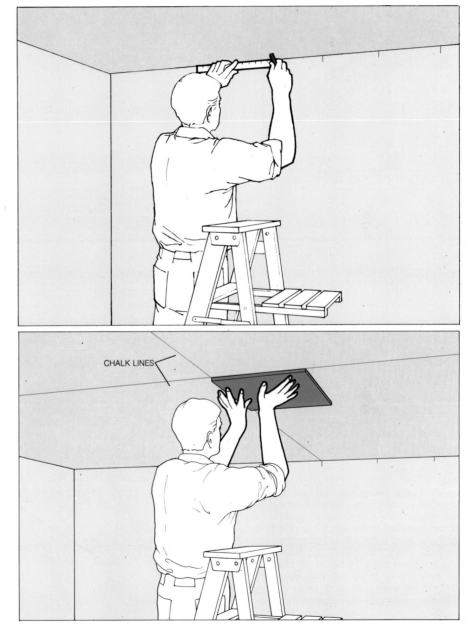

CHALK LINES

2 Applying the adhesive. With a wooden spatula or mastic gun, apply five walnut-sized blobs of adhesive to the back of a tile—one in each corner and one in the middle. Put the first tile in the centre of the ceiling where the chalk lines cross (above). Use one chalk line only as a guide to ensure that the tiles run straight along the axis of the room. To transfer some of the adhesive to the ceiling and help the tile to stick, press it into position with a sliding motion. Fix the remainder of the first row of tiles along the same chalk line, then fit the rest of the whole tiles in straight lines on either side of the first one. Check that the tiles lie evenly, applying more adhesive at the back if necessary. With an electrical outlet such as a ceiling rose, tile as closely as possible to it on two adjacent sides, then follow the instructions on page 78.

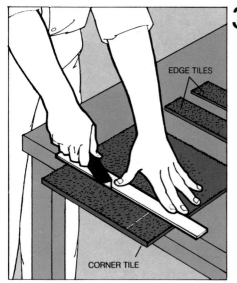

EDGE TILES

CORNER TILE

3 **Cutting edge and corner tiles.** When all the whole tiles have been fitted, measure the width of the gap between the wall and the outer edge of each tile in the nearest row. Use these measurements to cut edge and corner tiles individually: mark the required shape on each tile, using a sharp trimming knife and metal ruler, and cut it to fit. Stick each tile in place, starting with the corners.

If using tongue and groove tiles, trim off the tongue, or the upper edge of the groove, to enable you to slide the last row of tiles into place.

Cutouts for Electric Fittings

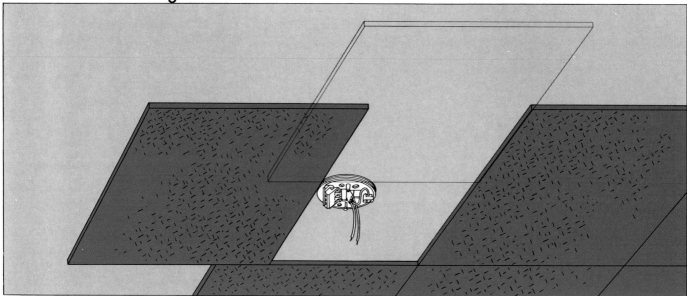

1 **Tiling round a ceiling rose.** Having tiled as closely as possible to two adjacent sides of the ceiling rose, slide a fresh tile alongside a tile already installed on one side of the rose. Slide the loose tile up to the rose and mark the tile at the point where it touches the midpoint of the rim, but do not mark the face of the tile. Slide the same tile up to the adjoining side of the rose and mark the point on the tile's adjacent side where it touches the midpoint of the rim.

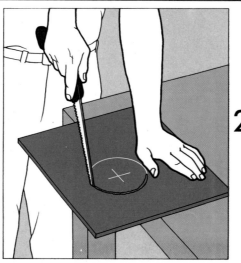

2 **Trimming the tile.** Using a steel square, extend the marks on the sides of the tile. The point at which these lines intersect on the back of the tile marks the centre of the ceiling rose. Transfer the centre mark to the face of the tile. Set a pair of compasses to a measure slightly less than the radius of the rose. Draw a circle on the face of the tile with the centre of the circle at the point you have marked. Using a compass saw held with the blade pointing outwards at a slight angle, make a bevelled cut round the circle through the face to the back of the tile. Glue the tile in place round the ceiling rose.

Installing and Lighting a Suspended Ceiling

A suspended ceiling, made of removable panels supported by a grid, enables you to lower the height of a room, conceal pipes and other unsightly fixtures, and to unify rooms which have been joined together to make a larger living space.

The grid consists of long main runners and shorter cross Ts made of aluminium or galvanized steel with an aluminium finish, suspended from the ceiling by hanger wires. The spacing of the grid depends on the size and shape of the ceiling panels— they can be either 300 or 600 mm square, or 1200 by 600 mm. Runners are sold in varying lengths, with holes for hanger wires every 50 to 75 mm, and slots for cross Ts every 100 mm.

Ceiling panels are manufactured in a wide range of materials and finishes. There are two basic methods of installation: the first is to rest the panels on top of the framework which is then visible below, as shown here and overleaf for 1200 by 600 mm panels. The alternative is to interlock the panels with the grid, concealing the framework and giving the appearance of a continuously tiled ceiling. The second method is commonly used with acoustic or mineral fibre tiles.

The outer edges of the suspended ceiling are supported by edge framing, which is fixed to the wall. If the old ceiling is made of plasterboard on timber ceiling joists, the runners are usually hung at right angles to the joists. On a concrete ceiling, fix the main runners across the shorter dimension of the room, using metal anchor bolts with built-in screw eyes to hold the wires.

Before beginning the work, plan the position of the runners and cross Ts carefully, ensuring that you have cut tiles of equal size on opposite sides of the room *(page 80)*. Building regulations on ceiling levels vary, but most local authorities suggest a minimum room height of 2.3 metres.

New lighting is easily accommodated in a suspended ceiling. Fluorescent fixtures can be fitted to the old ceiling behind translucent suspended panels or set into the new grid as fluorescent panels. However, the simplest method is to fit recessed spotlights in the new ceiling tiles. After choosing the location of the new lights, have old wiring repositioned if necessary, and consult an electrician if you are concerned about any extra load on the system. Three 100 watt bulbs will normally be sufficient for a 16 square metre ceiling. In Australia and New Zealand all wiring jobs should be undertaken by a licensed practitioner.

1 Measuring ceiling height. Mark the proposed ceiling height—allowing room below the joists to clear ducts, pipes or other obstructions—on the wall at the corners of the room. In each corner drive a nail into the wall at the level marked. Stretch a chalk line tautly between the nails, and snap the line across each wall.

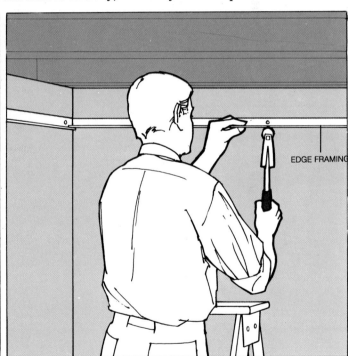

2 Installing edge framing. Screw or nail edge framing into the studs or masonry along each wall at ceiling height. If an irregularity in the wall causes the framing to bow, slacken the screw until the framing is straight, then shim any spaces left behind it with small pieces of wood or foam, and make good with filler. Where the ends of two strips of framing meet at a corner, lap one end over the other.

3 **Positioning runners and cross Ts.** To ensure a symmetrical arrangement of the panels, start by marking the centres of the walls at ceiling level. Since the short ends of the panels will abut the walls parallel to the joists, these walls must be divided into centred 600 mm intervals. Measure from centre to corner, and determine the distance in millimetres beyond the last full panel. If this surplus is 300 mm or more *(right, above)*, snap a chalk line across the joist bottoms from the centre of one wall to the centre of the other. If the surplus is less than 300 mm, mark the ceiling along a line 300 mm to one side or the other of the midpoints *(right, below)*. In either case, mark across the ceiling at 600 mm intervals on both sides of the first line.

To centre the long dimension of the panels on the walls perpendicular to joists, measure in the same way from centre to corner. The surplus is the distance to the corner from the last mark. If the surplus is 600 mm or more *(right, above)*, plan to space cross Ts at 1200 mm intervals on both sides of the centre mark. If the surplus is less than 600 mm *(right, below)*, plan to space cross Ts from points 600 mm on either side of the centre mark. Finally, mark the walls above the edge framing for cross Ts.

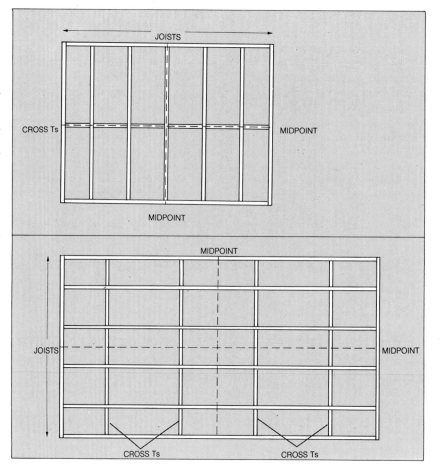

Hanging the Frame

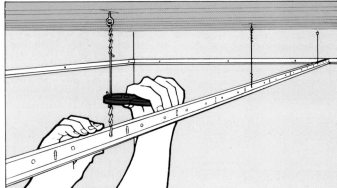

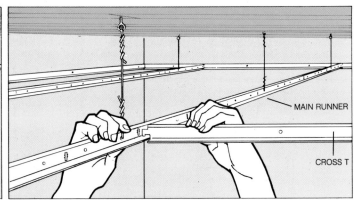

1 **Attaching runners.** Along the lines marked across the joists, attach a screw eye to the bottom edge of every other joist or, for a concrete ceiling, use anchor bolts at 400 mm intervals. Insert a hanger wire in each eye, secure the wires by twisting and bend the free ends to a 90-degree angle. Align the cross-T slots with the marks you have made above the edge framing *(Step 3, above)*; add lengths of runners as needed and cut off the excess. Set each runner in place with its ends resting on the edge framing. Thread hanger wires through the holes in the runners. Level each runner by adjusting the hanger wires, then secure each wire by twisting it round itself.

2 **Connecting the cross Ts.** Connect the runners with cross Ts at the proper intervals by fitting the ends of the cross Ts into the slots in the runners; check with the manufacturer's instructions to ensure that the frame is correctly assembled. Along the two walls perpendicular to the joists, rest the outer ends of the cross Ts on the edge framing.

Completing the Ceiling

Inserting the panels. Install panels in all the full-sized openings in the grid. Lift each panel diagonally up through the framework, turn it to the horizontal and rest its edges on the flanges of the runners and the cross Ts. Check the alignment of full-sized panels and grid, then trim panels to fit the smaller spaces round the border of the grid and install them.

Light Fittings for a Suspended Ceiling

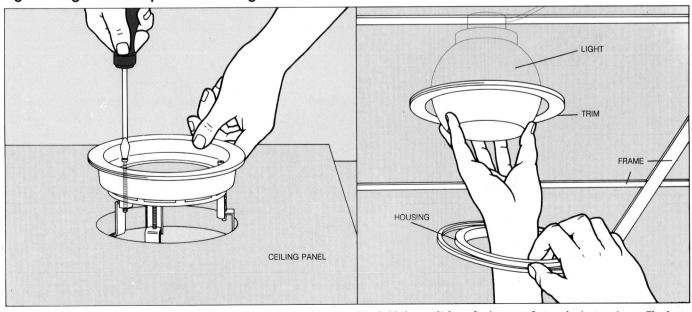

CEILING PANEL

LIGHT

TRIM

FRAME

HOUSING

Installing recessed spotlights. Before starting work, check that the relevant electrical circuit is dead—by removing the fuse or by switching off at the mains. Take a ceiling panel that will hold a light and find the centre by drawing two diagonals on the back of the panel. Draw a circle from the centre just big enough to hold the spotlight housing. Cut out the hole using a compass saw.

Place the light housing in the hole, tightening the fixing clamps on the panel so that it is secure *(above, left)*. Lift the panel into the frame and connect the light unit to the existing wiring, following manfacturer's instructions. Check to make sure that the light is working, then slide the unit into the housing and secure it. Fit the trim to complete the installation. Repeat this operation for the other lights, then install the remaining ceiling panels.

5

A roof with a view. A prefabricated window can be simply installed in a roof using basic carpentry techniques. The frame of wood with aluminium cladding is fixed to the roof structure with metal angle brackets; weatherproof flashing slots neatly over the outside of the frame to keep the window watertight. The double-glazed sash, held at each side by centrally placed hinges, swings through 180 degrees for ease of cleaning and maximum ventilation.

In most houses, the largest unused space is that immediately below the roof—the attic. It is an area which can be adapted to fulfil a variety of needs for additional space, whether for occasional use, storage or extra living accommodation. Because you are not building outside the existing structure, it is also a comparatively straightforward and inexpensive means of extending your home.

One of the first things you have to decide is how you want to use your attic—a decision which may depend on your local authority's building regulations. Any structural work necessary to make your roof space usable has to be submitted to the authority for approval. If you have opted for creating a permanent living area in the roof, the regulations are strict: a fixed staircase will have to be installed and, if the conversion effectively adds a storey to a house that has two or more already, extra fire prevention measures must be taken throughout the house.

As many of these regulations do not apply to the creation of non-habitable space, you may find that a simple conversion is a more viable proposition. With a minimum of structural alteration, and little or no disruption to the rest of the house, you can create an area for occasional use as a hobbies room, dayroom, workroom or store—a simple conversion well within the capabilities of a competent amateur builder.

The other important consideration on which your plans will depend is the structure of the roof itself *(pages 84–85)*. Familiarize yourself thoroughly with the design of your roof before making any detailed plans. If you think that the structure needs to be altered in order to make the conversion, seek professional advice.

The major tasks of loft conversion—providing light and access—have been made much easier by the development of factory-produced roof windows and lightweight retractable loft ladders. Both come in a range of sizes and models, suitable for most situations, and are supplied ready for installation. All you need to do is to provide the opening in the floor or roof covering to fit them *(pages 88–89 and 92–97)*.

A simple conversion is completed by adding a floor, ceiling and walls to the new attic space. Begin by making sure the existing attic joists are strong enough to support an increased load *(page 90)*. For an unheated storage area, you then only need to lay flooring on top of the existing insulation *(page 91, top)*. For a complete room with a soundproof floor, begin by building the framework for the walls and ceiling *(pages 98–99)*, then lay a "floating" floor *(page 91, below)*, before finishing the walls and ceiling with plasterboard.

The Anatomy of a Roof: the Skeleton under the Skin

One of the more complicated structures of a house is immediately under the bland exterior of a pitched roof. It is a framework which must not only bear the weight of the roof covering—be it of tiles, slate or metal—but also redistribute the forces inherent in inclined planes. The design, shape and size of a house will all condition the way the roof skeleton is built and, to add further complications, there are often several solutions to the same problem—and these can vary from area to area, from country to country.

However, the fact that there may be several ways of tackling a roof design can be an advantage when it is necessary to change it—for example, to provide more living space. But any such restructuring should only be undertaken with a full understanding of the function of roof timbers, and usually with expert advice.

Seen in cross-section, the simplest form of a pitched roof is a triangle: the sloping members, or rafters, exert a downward and outward thrust which is counteracted by "tie" members fixed horizontally between them. The tie members, which also act as joists for the ceiling of the room or rooms below, may be supported by hangers from the ridge at the apex of the roof. This type

of pitched roof—called the single roof—can only be used for small spans of up to 5.5 metres, because the rafters have no means of additional support.

One variation is the collar roof, where the tie members, known as collars, are positioned up to one-third of the way up the rafters. Often found in more cheaply built houses, the collar roof extends the rooms below into the roof space, but at the expense of the attic.

A double roof is created by introducing purlins and their supports. These provide additional support for the rafters and help redistribute the roof's load (below, and opposite page, top left). The many variations of this kind of roof, which is common in terraced and semi-detached housing, can adequately span up to 7.5 metres.

A triple roof (opposite page, bottom left) consists of three layers of timbers, and is common in houses built before the middle of the 19th century. The innermost layer consists of sturdy triangular trusses framed together and positioned at 2.5 to 3-metre intervals along the length of the roof. The second layer is of purlins laid across the outside of the trusses; the third layer is the rafters, which support the roof covering, but serve no structural function.

The roofs of most modern houses are built from factory-made sections which are similar in design to their traditional counterparts, but made from smaller timbers. Known as trussed rafters, these perform a double function both by supporting the roof covering and bearing the load. Because they have to be positioned much closer together than in a roof of traditional design, a conversion is difficult. Also, they usually have a much lower pitch, leaving little or no space for headroom.

In addition to these structural variations, the design of the roof will depend upon the shape of the house, and whether it is detached, terraced or semi-detached. Where a house has gable end walls (that is, where the end walls are built up to the ridge of the roof), its roof will have a simple gable to gable cross-section. If the end walls are not built up, as in the case of a detached house, the roof will be sloped, or "hipped", to meet the walls. If the house is not built as a single square or rectangle, then the roof will change direction to cover the extension and will have valleys where two pitched surfaces meet.

All these variations will affect the number and distribution of additional supporting members in the attic space.

The framework of a roof. The double roof shown here illustrates the function of its timber supports. The inclined rafters are fixed to a ridge board at the apex of the roof and are tied horizontally by tie members, or joists. The joists also support the ceilings of rooms below. Both rafters and joists rest on wall plates running on top of the inner edge or leaf of the exterior walls. Horizontal beams called purlins provide intermediate support for the rafters. To give extra support to the joists, vertical timbers called hangers are fixed at regular intervals between them and the rafters near the purlins or the ridge. Binders crossing the joists at the feet of the hangers spread support evenly between joists. Where joists rest on an intermediate load-bearing wall (page 56), weight from the purlins can be transferred to the wall via inclined members called struts, fixed at regular intervals. The struts are attached to a binder which spreads the weight evenly along the wall. Horizontal ties, which counteract the outward thrust of the rafters, are often fixed between the rafters either above or below the purlins.

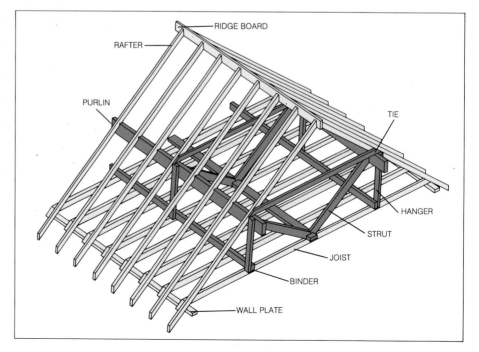

RIDGE BOARD
RAFTER
PURLIN
TIE
HANGER
STRUT
JOIST
BINDER
WALL PLATE

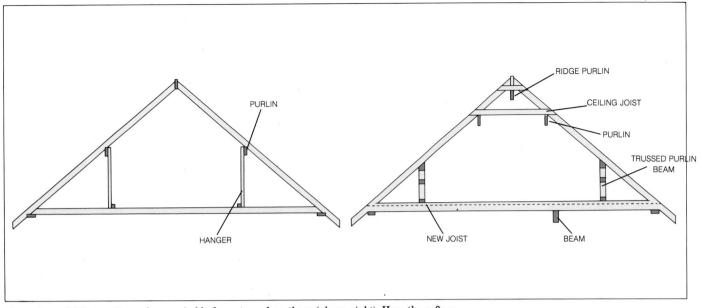

The purlin roof. Most purlin roofs are suitable for conversion. In terraced housing the purlins, positioned midway along the rafters, are supported at both ends by load-bearing walls. Hangers fixed next to the purlins help support the joists *(above, left)*. In large roofs of this kind it may be possible to build walls in front of purlins and hangers without disturbing them, but often they occupy space needed for windows. If they must be removed, a combination of supports may be needed to replace them *(above, right)*. Here the rafters are supported in two places: trussed purlin beams run from wall to wall at a low level and, higher up, new purlins are installed. To give maximum headroom these purlins are fitted below the level of the ceiling joists. At the apex of the roof, a ridge purlin helps to eliminate outward thrust. New joists support the conversion and, as there is no intermediate load-bearing wall, a beam is installed under them to take the load.

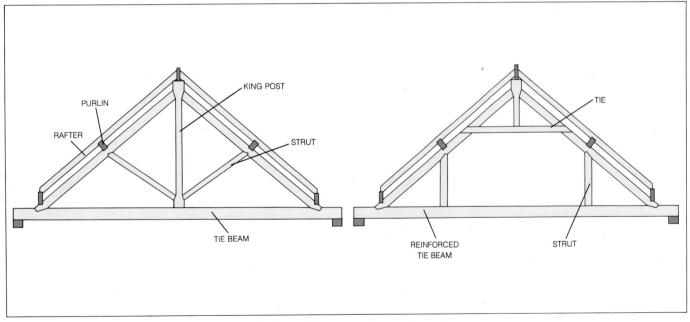

The triple roof. The traditional trussed or triple roof is easily converted. The spaces between trusses are usually big enough for rooms and, in larger roofs, doorways fit comfortably beneath struts. The interior truss members, here a king post and struts *(above, left)*, can be kept as a decorative feature or concealed within dividing walls. Where it is necessary to remove truss timbers, alternative support must be provided. Here *(above, right)*, the inclined struts are replaced with vertical ones. The king post is cut back to ceiling level and horizontal ties installed. The tie beam, which supports floor joists spanning between trusses, is reinforced to take the extra load.

Planning a Simple Attic Conversion

In planning an attic conversion, the major limitation is the structure of the roof itself. An examination of the inside of the attic will reveal how suitable it is for conversion *(page 84)*. Sometimes, it is possible to fit a room between structural timbers and even to incorporate them into the design of the room, but often some alteration to the roof timbers is unavoidable.

In either case, begin by measuring the attic space *(opposite page, Step 3)*, and then make a rough scale plan to ensure that you will gain enough space to make the conversion worthwhile. Use felt-tipped pen to make your marks on the joists and rafters, as this will save having to repeat the process at a later stage. If the plan shows that there is room to fix a ceiling at a normal height over about half the floor area, a conversion should yield a well-proportioned room. If not, or if any alteration to the roof timbers is necessary, you should consult an architect or a specialist.

Having resolved this problem, plan the rest of the conversion using the scale drawing. First, mark on the plan existing structural features, such as the access hatch and any windows; then add fixtures such as the water tank. With these in mind, mark out the provisional perimeters of the room. You are now in a position to make the all-important decisions about how to provide light and access to the new attic room.

There are three sorts of windows suitable for attics—dormer windows, roof skylights and windows in gable ends. Putting in a dormer window will provide extra space, but it will alter the appearance of the house, and will involve planning permission from your local authority. It is also a major operation involving substantial modification to the structure of the roof—a job that generally needs to be undertaken by a specialist builder.

Installing a roof skylight is a far more straightforward procedure *(pages 92–97)*, and allows a wide choice of positions. Gable end windows are also relatively easy to put in, but only providing there is no chimney breast in the wall.

Once you have decided on the position of the window, consider the location of the access opening into the attic. The determining factors will be the location of the planned window, the layout of the rooms below, and your choice between a fixed staircase and a retractable loft ladder. Because a fixed staircase is complicated to install and subject to strict building and fire regulations, it is best left to professionals. A retractable loft ladder, on the other hand, is compact, relatively easy to put in, and will give you a more flexible choice about its positioning. For safety, a railing can be fixed round the opening hatch.

Once you have finalized your plan, you can start on the necessary preparatory work. Work out how you are going to install services such as electricity, and plan the relocation of the water storage tank and any other fixtures. Check that the roof is sound and watertight, and replace broken tiles or slates, and damaged flashing. Make sure that the roof timbers are free of damp and decay. Treat mild outbreaks of woodworm, but if the damage is severe, consult a professional.

Start your actual conversion by providing access to make it easier to get materials into the attic. The strengthening of the floor and the installation of the window should then be completed before the erection of the walls. Finish by installing the floor and ceiling.

A room in the attic. To establish the position of the framework for the proposed room, draw lines across the rafters on either side of the attic at a height of 2.4 metres: installing joists at this height will produce a finished ceiling at a height of 2.3 metres. Below, at a height of 1.2 metres, draw a second line: this marks the position of the knee walls which form the outer perimeter of the room. The sloping rafters between the knee walls and the ceiling will be covered with plasterboard when the framework is lined *(page 74)*. The purlins, struts and binder will be removed and replaced with alternative structural supports *(page 85)* before you start work on the conversion.

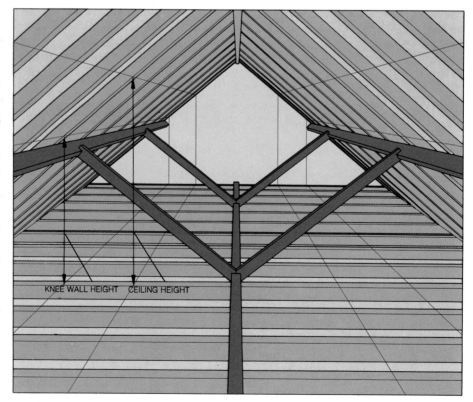

KNEE WALL HEIGHT   CEILING HEIGHT

Making a Plan of the Attic

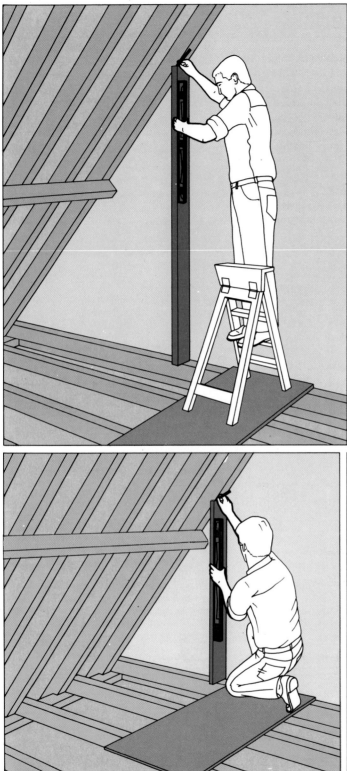

1 **Marking ceiling height.** From a length of straight-edged timber, cut a batten to the height of your ceiling, plus any floor insulation and covering. Working from a ladder placed on a board set across the joists, position the batten against the end wall, between the end rafter and joist beneath. Using a spirit level, check that the batten is vertical, then mark the rafter above the batten, and the joist beneath, with a felt-tipped pen. Using the batten and spirit level, transfer this mark to all the remaining rafters. Check the height of each mark to make sure that the whole ceiling reaches the minimum height, and raise all the marks if necessary. Then, with the batten and spirit level, mark all the joists vertically below the marks on the rafters.

2 **Marking the knee walls.** Trim the batten to the height of your knee walls. Working from a board placed across the joists, close to the rafters, hold the batten vertically in position against the end wall and mark the first rafter, transferring the mark to the other rafters and joists as before.

3 **Measuring the space.** Measure the length and width of the attic and draw a scale plan. Starting on one side of the attic, work across, measuring between the rows of marks. Transfer these measurements to your plan; you can then calculate the area of floor space with full ceiling height, and the area with a sloping ceiling.

A Space-Saving Method for Attic Access

A loft ladder is a good practical solution to attic access—compact, functional and easy to install. Modern loft ladders are retractable, either sliding or folding into the attic when not in use. Some of them come complete with a hatch lining and trap door or, if not, usually with instructions for lining the attic opening, making a door and finishing with architrave.

Folding ladders *(opposite)* usually have three sections connected by hinges which allow the ladder to be folded up. They are, however, usually larger than other loft ladders, and heavier—so, even though they are simple to fix in place, you may need an assistant. Sliding ladders consist of two or three sections which nestle on top of each other when stored. They fit into openings between 550 and 750 mm long, and 400 and 500 mm wide. When the hatch is opened, they unfold under their own weight, and are secured by sliding catches. Made to fit into spaces as small as 350 by 300 mm, the concertina ladder is the lightest and most compact, but not the sturdiest. It is made from a series of hinged cross-members, like trellis work, with steps fitted between. With all ladders you have to make sure there is space in the attic to accommodate the ladder when it is folded away. Sliding ladders fold in an arc and need even more roof space.

It may be possible to install the ladder without any change to the existing hatchway. If not, you can either cut a new opening, or enlarge the existing one—the basic procedure is the same. To make a new opening, begin by marking the area to be removed, remembering to allow for the thickness of the trimmers, and lining or frame. If the ceiling is lath and plaster, score along the marked lines with a trimming knife, chip away the plaster, then saw through the laths and remove them. To frame the opening, fit trimmers between the existing joists. Where a joist crosses the opening, which will often be the case if the joists are at 400 mm centres, you must remove it before fitting the trimmers. If the opening does not extend to the full width between joists, fit a false joist between the trimmers, using the technique shown on page 94, or enlarge the opening to the next joist, as shown here.

1 **Cutting a hole in the ceiling.** Locate a joist running to one side of the area to be removed *(page 10)*, then make a hole in the ceiling next to it, using a trimming knife. Check there are no cables above, then, using the joist as a guide for one side, mark out the outline of the opening on the ceiling. Cut through the plasterboard along the side of the joist with a saw, then score along the remaining marked lines with a trimming knife so you can break out the plasterboard.

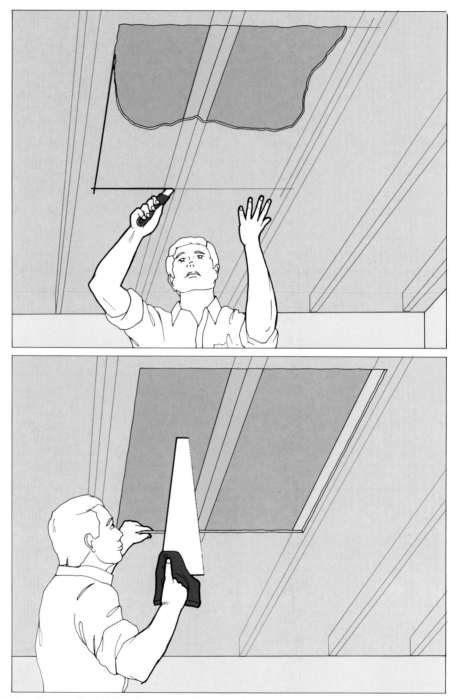

2 **Removing a section of joist.** If you are cutting a large opening, position adjustable props between floor and ceiling on either side of the hatchway outline to support the joists until the trimmers are in position *(page 60)*. Saw through the joist at either side of the opening, making sure that you keep the cut square, and remove the cut section.

3 **Fixing the trimmers.** Cut trimmers to fit between the joists on either side of the opening, using timber the same size as the joists, and position the trimmers flush with the underside of the joists. Using 100 mm round-wire nails, fix the trimmers by nailing through the joists into the trimmer ends, and also by nailing through the trimmers into the cut joist ends. Cut two strips of plasterboard to cover the underside of the trimmers, fix them with plasterboard nails, and make good the joints *(page 46)*.

Fitting a Loft Ladder

A combined ladder and hatch. An all-in-one loft ladder and hatch kit *(right)* consists of a preformed frame with a hatch door and folding ladder. Once the opening in the ceiling is prepared, the unit can be set in place and secured with screws or adjustable fixing springs. Ladder kits are large and solid, often needing openings up to 1100 mm long by 570 mm wide. If the geography of the room below means you have to position the opening lengthwise across the joists, you may have to cut out two of them. To operate the ladder, open the hatch door using the lever; with the aid of a gas piston the door will open back and the ladder will slowly unfold. When fully extended, the ladder locks into position.

A Groundwork for Attic Rooms

The simplest way to lay a new floor in an attic is to put down tongue and groove chipboard sheets *(pages 68–69)*. The 2440 by 610 by 18 mm sheets will go through most access hatches and can be laid straight on top of the joists, or raised off them for improved soundproofing *(opposite page)*.

The attic conversion will add to the load on the joists, which are already carrying a ceiling below, so examine the joists to see if they are strong enough and properly spaced. (This can be checked in your local building regulations which give the recommended size, span and spacing for floor joists.) Also, use a long straightedge and a spirit level to check that the joists are even enough for a new floor.

In the event of any deficiency, new joists placed alongside the existing ones will have to be installed. If they are attached to the wall plate at a slightly higher level, as shown here, they will bear the weight of the new room without putting additional strain on the ceiling of the room below.

New joists can run directly between exterior walls, or between exterior and interior load-bearing ones *(page 56)*, though, in some cases, you may have to remove tiles above the eaves to get the new joists in. Reinforce long spans between exterior walls by fixing horizontal struts between the joists to prevent them from twisting *(right, below)*. Short span joists can be hung from purlin beams, or otherwise supported by the roof structure. Joists between party walls can be fixed in metal hangers. You may have to make room for new joists by relocating intermediate roof timbers *(page 85)*, but this should not be attempted without professional advice.

You can lay the floor before or after the walls are built but, if you lay the floor first, the sole plates for the walls are fixed to the joists through the chipboard. If you want a storage area behind the walls, lay the chipboard up to the eaves *(opposite, above)*.

To give a heated attic room the benefit of warmth from the rest of the house, remove any existing insulation between the joists before laying the floor. For an unheated storage area, leave the insulation in place. To reduce noise from the attic, the floor can be "floated" *(opposite, below)*.

New Supports for a Level Floor

1 Levelling the joists. Measure the span of the existing joists and cut new ones to fit. Cut the ends to the same angles as the roof slope. With a spirit level on a long straightedge, find the joist at the highest point of the attic. Fix packing approximately 12 mm thick to the wall plate alongside both ends of this joist, using 25 mm lost-head nails. Slide a new joist into position over the packing pieces, inserting more packing if necessary to make sure that it is level. Toe-nail the joist ends to the wall plates with 75 or 100 mm round-wire nails, and fix the new joist to the old one with 75 mm No. 8 screws spaced at 400 mm intervals. Lay the straightedge and spirit level across the joists, resting one end on the new joist. Working at the other end of the straightedge, install a second new joist, making sure that it is level with the first. Repeat the process to cover the entire floor area, fitting all the new joists to the level of the first two.

PACKING

2 Fixing strutting. Mark the mid-points along the span of the new joists. Beginning at one end of the room, measure and cut 50 by 50 mm timbers to fit between the new joists, which will usually be about 100 mm deeper than the old ones. Fit each one in place with one end resting on an old joist. Fix this end with a 100 mm round-wire nail from the other side of the new joist. Toenail the other end with 75 mm nails. Work across the room in this way.

A Fixed Platform Floor

Arranging chipboard sheets. Starting at one side
of the attic under the eaves, work out a pattern
for the sheets, with the long edge at right angles
to the joists. Avoid alignment of joints, and use
as many whole sheets as possible. If new joists
have been laid alongside the old ones *(opposite)*,
fix the sheets using lost-head nails at 150 to
200 mm intervals along each new underlying
joist. Where flooring is to be laid directly on to
joists into which the ceilings of the rooms below
are fixed, you should use 44 mm No. 8 screws to
avoid damaging the plaster beneath.

A "Floating" Soundproof Floor

Assembling the layers. After the walls are installed, lay 25 mm thick, high-density glass fibre
insulation matting loosely over the joists. Allow
an extra 25 to 50 mm all round the room for
turning up the walls. Cut 50 by 50 mm timber
battens to run along the tops of the joists, and
nail them temporarily in place. Work out a pattern for the flooring sheets as before, allowing for
them to be pushed tightly up to the insulation
against the walls. Beginning at one side of the
room, lay the sheets across the joists *(right)*, removing as you go the nails holding the battens in
place. Fix each sheet to the underlying battens
using 50 mm lost-head nails, which should not
penetrate through to the insulation. When all
the sheets have been laid, trim any insulation
material above the floor, and fix skirting, bedded
on a thin cork strip, round the room.

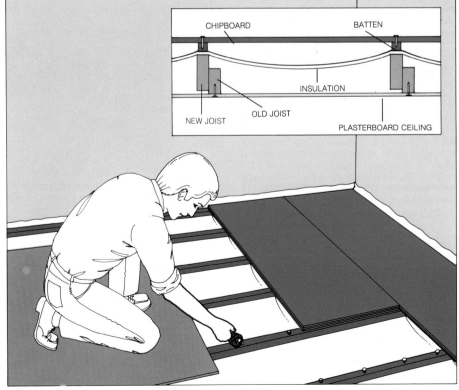

Bringing Light to the Attic Space

The simplest way to ventilate and light an attic is to install a skylight window. These were once simple top-hinged windows used mainly for aeration, but today they are stylish units intended to enhance habitable rooms, and are supplied complete from a factory ready for installation. Because they are designed to lie flush with the existing roof covering, no major structural alteration is required.

Unless your house is a listed building, or is situated within a conservation area, you will not require planning permission, as there will be no dramatic change in the external appearance of the house. But if the installation is part of a complete conversion, you must first submit your plans to your local authority.

Factory-made roof windows are available in sizes varying between 700 by 550 mm to 1400 by 1340 mm and they are suitable for roof pitches between 15 and 85 degrees. The window itself usually has a wooden frame clad with protective aluminium, and is hinged in the centre to allow the sealed, double-glazed sash to pivot through 180 degrees to provide for maximum ventilation and easy cleaning.

The windows are supplied complete with metal flashing, which bridges the gap between the frame and the roof covering to make it watertight. The type of flashing used depends on your roof covering: thick, plain or profiled interlocking tiles need a different type from thinner coverings such as slates or felt. You will have to specify which type of flashing you need when you order your window and, if the pitch of your roof is very low, special adaptations to the flashing may be necessary.

Begin by working out the area of window needed to provide enough light. As a general guide, the total glazed area should be at least 10 per cent of the usable floor area of the attic room. Two smaller windows will often be easier to handle than one large one, and will probably look better as well.

To gauge the best height for the window, measure the pitch of the roof, then check the manufacturer's specifications: most recommend ideal heights and pitches for optimum visibility. Make sure you will not breach the health regulations by locating the window too close to a soil pipe. Once you have decided on the position of the window, the next step is to check that the rafters which will support it are sound.

Normally, the installation can be carried out from inside the roof, and an amateur should be able to complete the work in two days, provided he is well prepared in advance. If your roof tiles are bold profiled, you will need to hire an angle grinder to dress them in case their sharp edges damage the soft lead flashing. Have plenty of plastic sheeting to hand to cover the opening at night, or in case of rain.

If fitting the frame involves cutting back one or more rafters, as shown in this example, you should support the rafters above and below the sections to be removed before starting work. Use adjustable props *(page 59)*, which can be removed once the opening has been lined. As a final safety precaution, place warning signs at ground level before you commence work, in case any tools or materials are accidentally dropped from the roof.

A window in the rafters. The window shown here has a frame which is wider than the space between two rafters. The intermediate rafter which crosses the space the window will occupy is cut back and then supported top and bottom by trimmers nailed between the intact rafters. Here the trimmers have been positioned a few centimetres away from the frame to allow room for fitting the interior linings which will bridge the gap between the frame and the interior wall. The linings are splayed so they will fit horizontally at the top and vertically at the bottom *(inset)*. If, as here, the framing rafters are too far apart to support both sides of the frame, a false rafter is fitted vertically between the trimmers. The window frame is then fixed to the framing and false rafters with angle brackets. After the frame is installed, flashing is fitted around the edges, and held in place by metal frame profiles. The roof covering is replaced and the tiles are trimmed to fit the new opening, with a short tile course installed above the window, and the side tiles cut to fit neatly over the flashing. The window sash is then fitted into the frame.

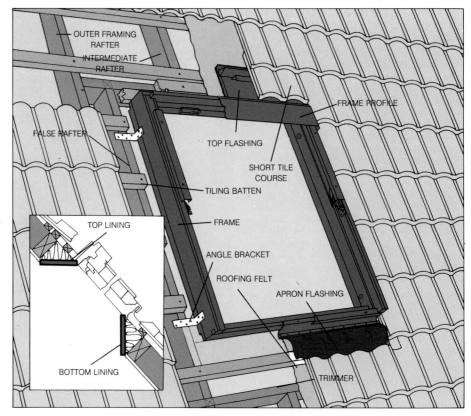

Fitting a Roof Window

1 **Marking the frame position.** Decide the position of the window, and mark where the bottom of the frame will come on the wide face of the framing rafter. Remove a patch of roofing felt to make sure the mark is level with the top of a tile course. Adjust the mark if necessary and square a line across the rafter at this point A *(inset)*. Measure the external height of the window frame, stripped of its profiles, and draw a second parallel line (B) on the rafter this distance from your first mark. Mark the thickness of the rafter up from line B and down from line A. Square lines across the rafter at these points *(CD and FG)*. To make allowance for the window lining, use a spirit level to draw a horizontal line from point D across the rafter to E, and draw a vertical line from point G to H. From points E and H, square lines back across the rafter. Using a spirit level, transfer these lines to the outer framing rafter and the intermediate rafter. Lines E and H are where the intermediate rafter will be cut.

2 **Removing the roof covering.** Cut away the roof felt in the proposed window area, and pin back any spare material. Then remove the roof tiles or slates, working from the centre out, by lifting the nibs carefully over the battens and sliding the tiles free. If any are nailed to the battens, prise them free or cut through the nails with a slate ripper. Remove all tiles or slates from an area slightly larger than that of the window.

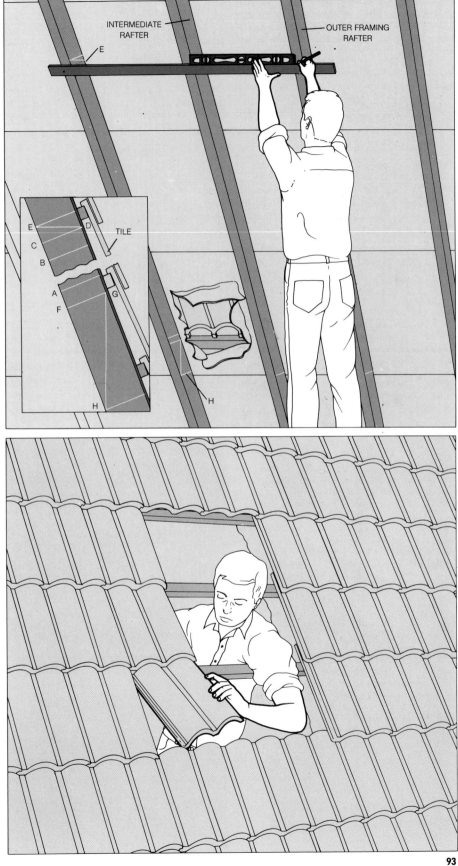

3 **Cutting away the intermediate rafter.** Saw through the intermediate rafter at the top and bottom of the opening along the marked cutting lines (E and H, Step 1), keeping the cuts square with the rafter. Using your free hand, support the weight of the timber as you make the second cut. Now remove the nails fixing the tiling battens to the rafter, taking care not to damage the battens, and remove the cut rafter section. The battens are not cut out at this stage because they can only be marked for accurate cutting after the window frame has been positioned.

4 **Installing the trimmers.** Measure the distance between the framing rafters at the top and bottom of the opening. Cut two trimmers from timber of the same dimensions as the rafters. Position the trimmers, making sure they are correctly aligned with the marks (E and H), and are level and square at the corners. Nail the trimmers on to the cut ends of the intermediate rafter and through the framing rafters into the trimmer ends. Use three 100 mm round-wire nails for each joint.

5 **Putting in a false rafter.** Measure the external width of the stripped window frame and, following manufacturer's instructions, add side clearances. Mark this distance along the trimmers starting from the original framing rafter *(right)*. Measure the vertical distance between the two marks and cut a false rafter to this length. Position the false rafter between the marks on the trimmers and check that it is properly aligned. Nail through the trimmers into the ends of the false rafter using three 100 mm round-wire nails to secure each joint.

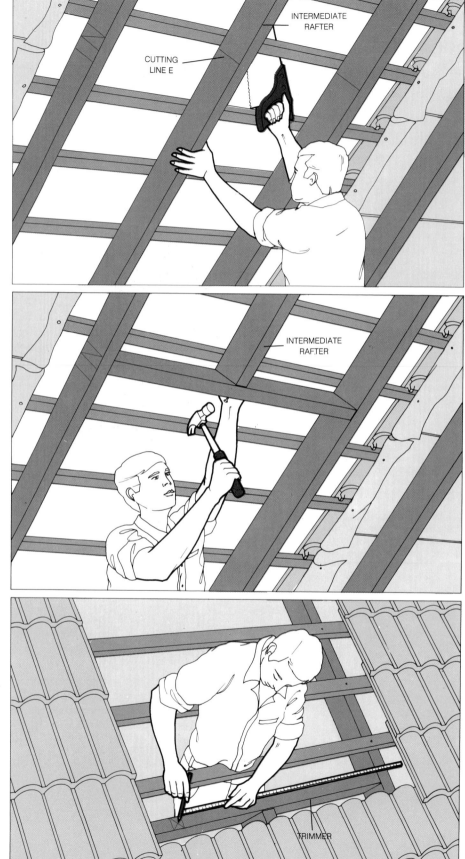

6 Positioning the frame. Cut out the central sections of the tiling battens in the opening, making a gap big enough to pass the frame through sideways. Replace the tile course below the opening and tack a piece of wood across the framing rafters as a spacer bar at the required distance between the window frame and the roof covering. Pass the frame through the gap and seat it on the spacer bar. Measure and mark the specified clearance between the frame and the roof covering on the tiling battens at either side of the frame *(right)*. Now mark the positions for the angle brackets on the adjoining rafters. To ensure that the frame sits at the right level in relation to the roof covering, adjust the bracket positions in accordance with the manufacturer's instructions, then screw them in place on the frame.

7 Trimming the battens. Remove the frame and pass it back through the gap into the attic. Cut back the battens along the marked lines, taking care not to damage them. Using a tile cutter or sharp pincers, trim any rough edges off the tiles below the opening. Tiles with a pronounced profile should be removed from the roof and their edges smoothed with an angle grinder.

8 Securing the frame. Set the frame back in position on the spacer bar. Hold the frame in place with a single screw in the brackets on the top left and lower right of the frame. Re-check the side clearances. Make sure that the frame is perfectly square by checking that the measurements of the diagonals are equal *(right)*. Fix the frame firmly in place using all four brackets and, finally, remove the spacer bar.

SPACER BAR

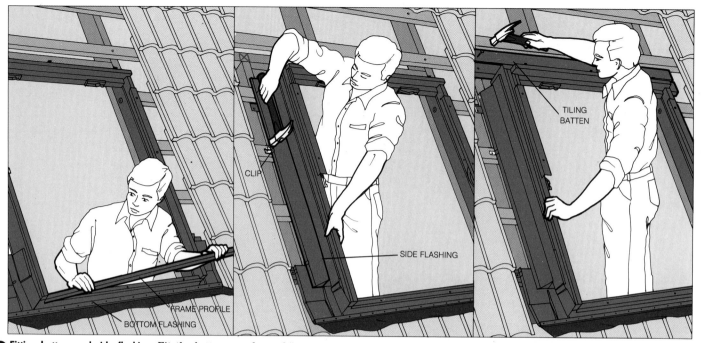

9 **Fitting bottom and side flashing.** Fit the bottom flashing and secure it, in this case by slotting the lower frame profile over the bottom of the window *(above, left)* and screwing it in place. The soft metal "apron" is to be left as it is until the rest of the flashing is completed. The next step is to fit the side flashings. In this example, they are fixed by nailing through adjustable clips into the adjoining tiling battens *(above, centre)*. Bridge the gap above the frame using tiling battens spaced at about 20 mm intervals: nail these into the adjoining rafters *(above, right)*.

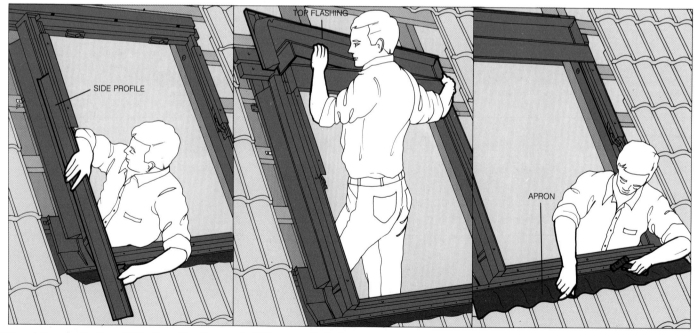

10 **Completing the flashing.** Slide the side frame profiles into place *(above, left)*, making sure that they cover the gap between the side flashing and the frame, then screw them into the frame. Attach the top profile in the same way, then install the top flashing making sure that the two fit together *(above, centre)*. With all the flashing in place check that it is secure and correctly fitted, and "dress" the soft metal apron. Using a lead dresser or a soft-faced hammer, work from side to side, carefully beating the metal until it lies flush with the roof tiles *(above, right)*.

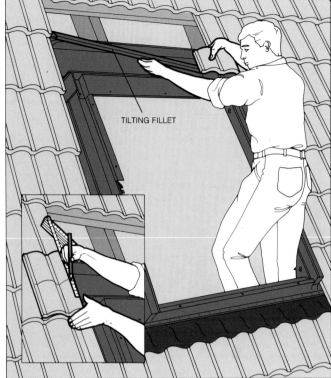

TILTING FILLET

11 **Replacing the side tiles.** Trim the tiles to fit, cutting them with an angle grinder if necessary. Working from the bottom up, replace the side tiles. With its nib over the batten, slide each tile under the adjacent one so that it locks in place. Ensure that the outer edges fit over the flashing.

12 **Fitting a short course.** To install a course of short tiles at the top of the frame, measure the gap and, allowing for overlap, cut the tiles to size *(inset)*. Fit a tilting fillet to support the short course; replace the tiles, alternating between the short course and the full one above.

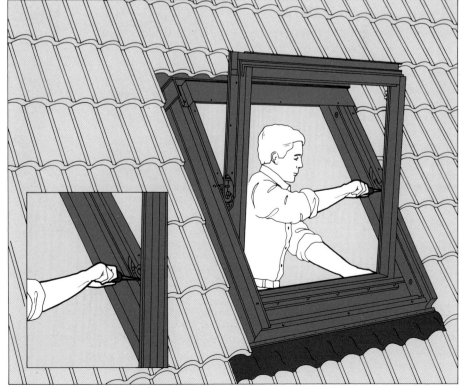

13 **Fitting the sash.** Hold the sash the right way up with the inside towards you. Rotate it through 180 degrees, so that it is wrong side out and upside down. With the sash held in this position, manoeuvre it into the frame opening. Align it so that the metal flange on either side of the sash connects with the frame hinges. Release the retaining screw in the frame hinge on either side, *(inset)*. Rotate the sash through 180 degrees, then check that the window opens and closes easily. If it does not, adjust all the screws and check that the sash is correctly aligned.

A Framework for Walls and Ceilings

The sloping roof of an attic creates special problems in building walls—problems that call for ingenious adaptations of conventional techniques. At ceiling height, usually 2.3 metres, joists are installed to convert two sloping surfaces to a single horizontal one. Where the partition wall is to be built, two joists attached one on each side of a single rafter provide a surface thick enough to attach the head plate of a conventional wall assembly (pages 36–39). At each end of these joists, rafters are thickened by additional timber to provide nailing surfaces for studs. Farther down the rafters, knee walls, usually 1.5 metres tall, convert a sloping surface to a vertical one. If your home pre-dates 1950, the rafters may be thicker than present-day timber. If so, use scrap timber to thicken the nominal 100 by 50 mm blocks between the joists. At the knee walls, simply centre the studs when you toenail them into the sole plate.

If the new room is to be comfortable, the completed framework must be insulated. The most suitable material is glass or mineral fibre wool, available in two forms. Mats come in long rolls; slabs in pre-cut rectangles, usually 600, 900 or 1200 mm long. Both come in widths that fit between joists or studs, and in varying thicknesses up to 160 mm. Install the thickest insulation you can fit between joists and studs.

Both mats and slabs can be purchased with a vapour barrier of chemically treated or foil-lined paper to stop the moisture-laden air of a heated room from penetrating the insulation material. Mats and slabs for use between studs and rafters usually come with stapling flanges at each side to make installation easier. Fit them with the vapour barrier facing inwards. Friction-fit slabs, usually used between floor joists, do not have flanges. Use slabs without a vapour barrier between the floor joists beyond the knee walls, taking care not to block ventilation at the eaves.

Cover the insulated wall and ceiling framework with plasterboard (pages 42–47 and 74–76); toenail noggings between the studs or rafters to provide a firm nailing surface at the junctions between the sloping rafters and the knee walls, and the sloping rafters and the ceiling. Finally, lay a "floating" floor (page 91).

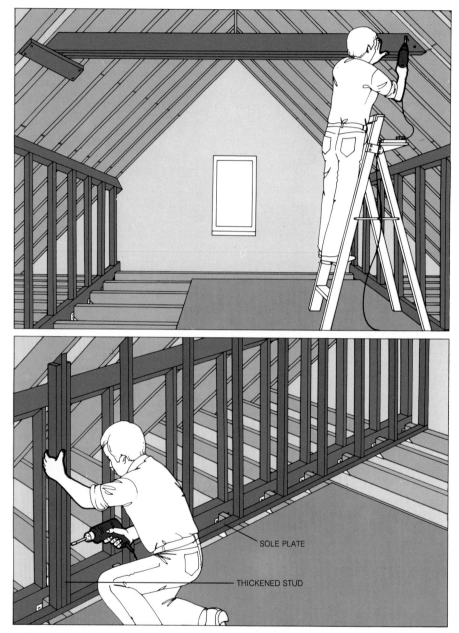

1 Installing ceiling joists. Mark the ceiling height (page 87, Step 1). Just below the marks, tack a 75 by 25 mm piece of timber across the rafter that will support the new wall, attaching it to the rafters on either side. Measure across the attic from roof to roof at the level of the marks. Cut two pieces of 100 by 50 mm timber 12 mm shorter than this distance, then cut the ends at the same angle as the slope of the rafter. Fix the joists to either side of the rafter, with the bottoms flush with the marks, leaving 6 mm between the joist ends and the roof covering (below); use two 75 mm No. 8 screws in each joint. If the span of the double joist exceeds 2.4 metres, nail 100 by 50 mm blocks between them at 900 mm intervals to stop them twisting. Fit single joists at ceiling height across the rest of the room in the same way.

SOLE PLATE

THICKENED STUD

2 Building knee walls. Measure across the marks on the joists for the knee walls (page 87) and cut two pieces of 100 by 50 mm timber to this length for the sole plates. Fix them with one 75 mm No. 8 screw into each joist. Place a length of 100 by 50 mm timber vertically between the sole plate and the rafter at the end of one wall. Trace the angle of the rafter on the timber and cut to this mark. Try this stud at the other end of the wall. If it fits, cut the remainder for that wall to the same length. If not, cut each individually. Fasten them to the rafters with 75 mm No. 8 screws, then toenail to the sole plate using 63 mm lost-head nails.

At the point where the partition wall is to be built between knee walls, thicken the end studs of the partition to make nailing surfaces for plasterboard. At the back of the end stud measure between the rafter and the top of the sole plate. Cut two pieces of 100 by 50 mm timber to this length and screw them either side of the stud with 75 mm No. 8 steel screws (above).

3 **Assembling the centre wall.** Measure the distance across the attic between the two thickened studs and cut a length of 100 by 50 mm timber to serve as the sole plate for the centre wall. Attach the sole plate to the joist with 75 mm No. 8 screws at 300 mm intervals, with the end of the plate meeting the inside end of the thickened knee wall stud. Measure the bottom of the double ceiling joist from rafter to rafter and cut a piece of 100 by 50 mm timber to this length for a head plate. Assemble this part of the wall as for a conventional partition *(pages 36–39)*, by nailing studs to the head plate, nailing the head plate to the double joist through the nailing blocks, and toenailing the studs to the sole plate.

To complete the wall, measure along the rafter from the end of the double joist to the top of the reinforced stud, and cut two pieces of 50 by 50 mm or 100 by 50 mm timber to that measurement. Screw these to opposite sides of the rafter, positioning the bottoms flush with the bottom of the rafter, using 75 mm No. 8 screws. Cut a 100 by 50 to run from the centre wall to the knee wall as a top plate; when you cut, angle one end to fit tightly against the knee wall stud. Nail the top plate against the thickened rafter.

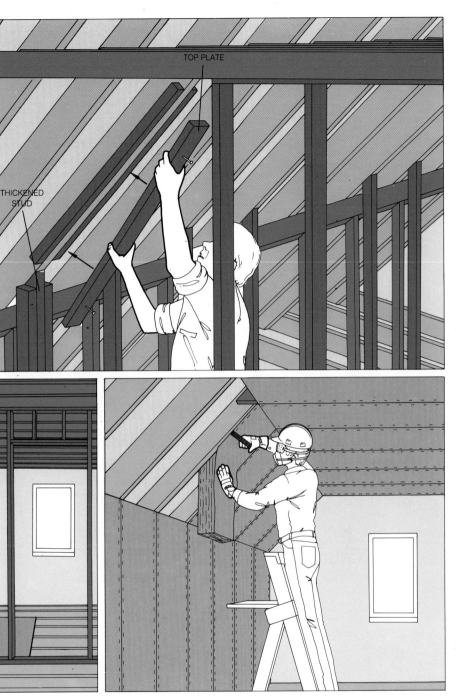

4 **Completing the centre wall.** Mark the centre wall sole plate for a stud next to the reinforced stud on the knee wall, and for additional studs at 400 or 600 mm intervals from that point to the end of the centre wall. Set lengths of 100 by 50 mm timber vertically on 100 by 50 mm scraps next to the marks, trace the height and angle of the rafter at the upper ends, and cut the timbers at the trace marks for studs. Toenail the studs into place between the top and sole plates with 63 mm lost-head nails; for a tight joint, fasten the first stud to the knee wall corner with 75 mm round-wire nails.

5 **Insulating walls and ceiling.** Fit insulation mats between knee wall studs. For the ceiling, cut mats to rafter-to-rafter measurements with about 50 mm extra on each end. Notch the ends to fit over the rafter, then staple the flanges to the ceiling joists at 150 mm intervals. To insulate between the rafters, select a mat or slab thickness that allows at least 12 mm of space between the insulation and the roof covering, so that air can circulate freely. Starting at the ceiling joists, staple the mats to the rafters as before. Allow a slight overhang at the bottom to fit behind the knee wall insulation. Use tape to cover the seams where the rafter insulation meets the ceiling and knee wall insulation.

6 Bringing in the Out-of-Doors

Supports for an opening. The rolled steel, reinforced concrete and timber lintels are used to support openings in load-bearing walls. Before breaking through the masonry, the weight must be redistributed on to props. Then the lintel area only is chipped out and the support beam is fixed into place, resting on bearings at either end. The plumb bob is used to sight precise and straight lines throughout the work.

A variant of Parkinson's law decrees that family living expands to fill all available space. A darkroom claims squatter's rights to the unused corner of the basement; the attic is converted into a playroom; the living room is partitioned off to create a separate dining area. Further expansion then depends on making use of outdoor space. Adding a wooden deck with a louvred or trellised covering, which opens from the kitchen or living room *(pages 108–113)*, provides a new arena that can be used for entertaining, barbecuing, dining or lounging during the warm months. And converting a garage *(pages 118–123)* produces a family activity room that can be used throughout the year.

Adapting an existing structure is far simpler than building an entirely new addition to the house—the heavy work of providing a roof, foundations and supports has already been done for you. Flooring over the concrete slab of a garage is like adding a wooden floor to a basement. In the case of the wooden deck, the frame is fixed securely to the existing structure of the house.

Building decks and converting garages usually involves taking down part of a load-bearing exterior wall in order to accommodate new doors and windows. Although breaking through such a wall requires time and careful planning, the techniques are not particularly difficult. Before you break through the masonry, however, you need to prop the wall to redistribute the weight of the building, and you must then install a lintel above the proposed opening. The damp-proof course must be replaced if it has been breached.

Once the opening is ready, the work of installing a door or window proceeds quickly with the aid of factory-assembled units. Carpenters used to construct windows from scratch, a job that involved joining well over a dozen parts for even a simple frame. Nowadays, however, doors and windows are obtainable pre-hung, with all their operating parts fixed in a jamb that only needs to be positioned and secured in the opening. A weatherproof sliding door, which comes complete with frame and runners, can be used to make a wooden deck or patio readily accessible to the rest of the house *(pages 106–107)*, and to integrate living space in and out of doors.

Breaking Through an Exterior Load-Bearing Wall

Breaking through an exterior wall requires the same techniques that are used for making a hole in an interior load-bearing structure, but it is a more complex procedure demanding very careful planning. Without proper consideration of the structure of the house, not only windows and doorframes but even interior walls can be pushed out of shape, seriously weakening the fabric of the building. Before you start work, you must determine what materials were used to build the wall, and whether it is a solid or cavity construction.

Planning the location of the opening can involve compromises. Inside the house you may want the new window or door to fit a certain decorating plan or a traffic pattern; outside, it may have to align with existing openings. If there are plumbing or electric lines at the location you have chosen, you must move them or choose a new location.

Finally, you must align the inside and outside plans for your opening. The easiest method is to measure an equal distance, inside and out, from an existing window or door. If the wall does not have a door or window, drill a pilot hole through the wall with a long masonry bit and use the hole as a reference point.

The technique of using adjustable steel props with scaffold boards to provide temporary support for an exterior wall is the same as that used for an interior one *(pages 59–60)*; the amount and type of propping and shoring that will be required depends on the size of your opening and the structure of your house *(below)*.

Permanent support for the exterior wall once the opening has been made is provided by a lintel which must be supported on sound, level bearings at each end. Lintels are made of concrete, lightweight pressed steel, rolled steel and timber, in sizes and shapes to suit all the different materials used in wall construction. The span of the opening, the load it must bear and the structure of the wall will determine the type of lintel you choose. For a cavity wall, you can use a specially designed boot-shaped lintel that supports both the inner leaf, which bears the majority of the weight, and the outer one.

Manufacturers and suppliers often offer free technical advice, but it is also important to consult a structural engineer regarding your plans. He will calculate the load or stress the lintel will be required to bear when installed. In addition, check that your planned alterations comply with local building regulations.

The lintel must be firmly mortared into the opening, on bearings at least 150 mm long at each end. Protection from fire is provided by covering the interior face of the lintel with plaster or plasterboard. Steel lintels should also be protected against corrosion with bituminous paint, and timber lintels should be treated with wood preservative.

Supporting the exterior walls of a house. The system of supports shown here is suitable for a typical two-storey house where an opening is to be made in a downstairs wall.

The upstairs window is held rigid with wooden shoring which braces the opening. The walls are supported with horizontal wooden needles and adjustable steel props *(pages 59–60)*. In this case both the upstairs and downstairs floor and ceiling joists are supported with adjustable props and scaffold boards that carry the weight through to the foundations.

Props should not be spaced more than 900 mm apart, so you may need to use more than two sets for your opening.

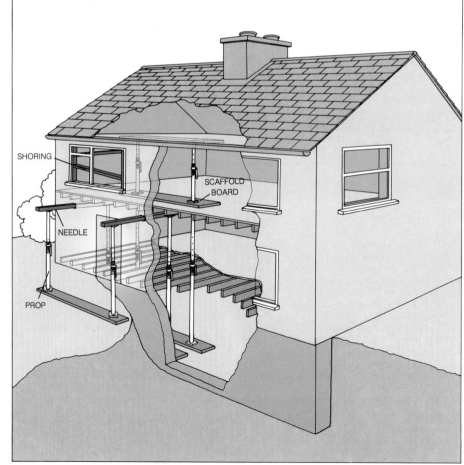

A Choice of Lintels

Concrete lintels. Reinforced or pre-stressed concrete lintels are suitable for openings of up to 4 metres in solid walls of brick, block or stone, or in cavity walls. They are manufactured in thicknesses that correspond to brick or block courses, and they come in a variety of widths and shapes. Pre-stressed lintels are lighter in weight than reinforced concrete and are easier to handle. They work in conjunction with the weight of the masonry immediately above them, and are only efficient if loaded to their full capacity. Reinforced concrete lintels are strengthened with steel rods. On the right a plank-shaped reinforced concrete lintel is correctly positioned in a solid brick wall with the rods at the bottom. For a cavity wall, you can use a reinforced concrete boot lintel *(far right)* in conjunction with a DPC.

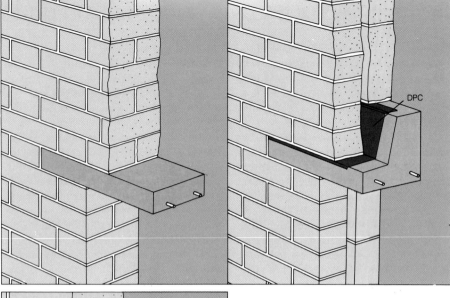

Steel beams. Steel beams, or rolled steel joists (RSJs) can carry much greater loads in relation to their sectional size than other types of lintel, and can be used to span openings of up to 6 metres. They are made in I-shaped sections in a range of widths and depths, but one of the disadvantages of these beams is that the sizes rarely correspond to the thickness of standard brick or block courses. For walls thicker than a single beam, two RSJs can be bolted together to support the load *(right)*. Another disadvantage of steel beams is that, because of their limited resistance to corrosion, they are not well suited to exterior walls.

An RSJ must be installed over a base of expanded metal lath, which provides a key for plaster. To finish and fireproof the inside of the opening, place timber wedges in the sides of the beam to provide a nailing surface for plasterboard, and cover the underside with plaster. For interior walls, build an enclosing wooden box and cover it with plasterboard.

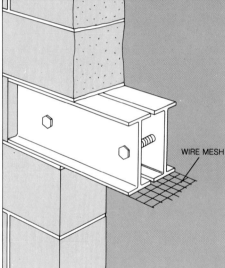

Lightweight steel lintels. The relatively high cost of pressed steel lintels is offset by their light weight and ease of use, making them a good choice for the amateur builder. Only fairly recently developed, they are available in sizes which span openings of up to 4.8 metres, and are made in a wide range of shapes to suit different building materials and wall structures. The steel boot lintel *(right)* is designed for a cavity wall. Like the concrete boot, it supports both leaves of the wall, but cannot be seen on the outside of the house. As it is made from water-resistant galvanized steel, it can be used without a DPC. The combination lintel *(far right)*, comprising a concrete plank or boot lintel and a lightweight steel lintel which supports the outer leaf, is suitable for both a cavity or brick-faced block wall. Insulation material can be placed between the two lintels to eliminate the passage of cold between the two leaves of the wall.

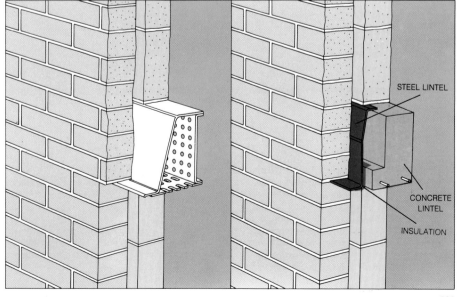

Techniques for a Cavity Wall: Cutting and Sealing the Gap

Making an opening in a cavity wall involves many of the techniques used for making an opening in a single-leaf load-bearing wall *(pages 59–63)*. Here, however, because of the difference in structure, a few refinements are necessary.

Cavity walls are made either of two brick leaves, or of one brick and one block leaf, and the leaves have a gap of between 50 and 150 mm between them. To prevent the passage of water through the wall, a vertical damp-proof course (DPC) must be installed at the sides of the opening to tie in with the existing horizontal DPC. Marking and cutting the opening has to be done first on the outer leaf of the wall, and then on the inner one at each stage. If the wall cavity has been insulated with loose fill, when you make the opening use battens the width of the cavity to retain the fill

until the sealing bricks are in place.

If the wall is load-bearing, prop the weight above before starting work *(page 102)*. You must also support the wall immediately above the opening while you cut the slot for, and install, the lintel.

Mark the position of the opening, including the lintel, as shown on page 59. Site the base of the opening on the horizontal DPC, usually about three brick courses above ground level, and try to make the sides of the opening coincide with lines of mortar joints. Then mark squares for the needle holes 200 mm above the top of the lintel *(page 60)*, and 150 mm in from each end. If the needle holes are more than 900 mm apart, you will have to cut a hole for a third, intermediate needle. Cut the needle holes in the outer leaf, then mark corresponding holes in the inner leaf by drilling

through it from the outside, using a long masonry bit. Cut out the inside holes, and slide the needles into place. Pack any gaps above the needles with slate or hardwood wedges, then tighten the props carefully *(page 59)*, using a spirit level to make sure that the needles are level.

Choose a suitable lintel for a cavity wall *(page 103)*. The dimensions of the slot that has to be cut to take the lintel will depend on the type you use; make sure you order one long enough for the opening plus 150 mm each end to rest on the bearings. Here, a boot-shaped lintel of galvanized pressed steel is used. Its weight and shape allow it to be lifted easily and inserted into the slot from inside the house. After installation, its hollow back is filled with a sand and cement mix, then covered with finishing plaster to match the rest of the room.

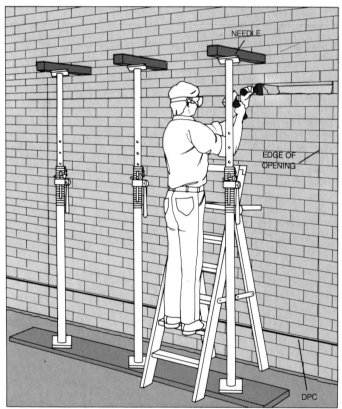

1 **Cutting the lintel slot in the outer leaf.** After installing the props and needles, remove the course of bricks marked for the lintel, using a jointing chisel, lump hammer and bolster. Extend the slot beyond the sides of the proposed opening by at least 150 mm. Transfer the lintel mark to the inner leaf of the wall by drilling through it at the bottom corners of each end of the slot with a long masonry bit.

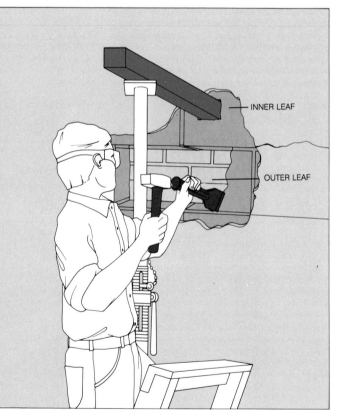

2 **Cutting the slot in the inner leaf.** Go inside the house and draw a line between the two drill holes. Using this as your base line, mark the height of the lintel and draw its outline on the wall. Remove the blocks or bricks within this outline. Then mark the vertical edges of the opening on the inside wall.

3 Installing a vertical DPC. Cut two lengths of 110 mm-wide DPC material to the height of the opening plus 500 mm. Working from inside the house, loosely roll up one strip. Holding the free end, push the roll into the cavity. Align the outer edge of the DPC with that of the bearing, then tack the free end to the inside wall. Install the second strip over the other bearing.

4 Installing the lintel. With a mix of 6 parts soft sand to 1 part cement, spread a 16 mm thick layer on the end bearings of each leaf, making sure that the mortar goes above and below the DPC strips. With a helper, lift the lintel into position with its front edge set back slightly from the face of the outer leaf *(inset)*. Check that the outside edges of the DPC strips are still aligned with the bear-ings. Fill the gap above the lintel on the inner leaf with mortar. From the outside, replace the line of bricks: spread mortar along the front edge of the lintel and on the top and sides of each brick before sliding it into position. Allow the lintel to settle for at least three days before continuing, then knock out the opening following the instructions on page 61, Step 8.

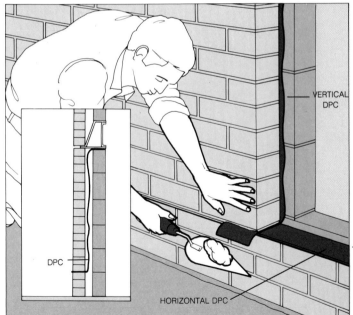

5 Tying in the DPC. Trim the opening *(page 61, Step 9)*. At the bottom on one side, carefully remove the brick sitting on the horizontal DPC. Unroll the vertical DPC so that it hangs down inside the cavity. Place its loose end on top of the horizontal DPC and mortar the brick back in place. Trim the DPC flush with the wall, top and bottom. Repeat on the other side of the opening.

6 Bricking up the cavity. Cut bricks to fit inside the cavity at the sides of the opening, allowing for 10 mm mortar joints between them. Mortar both the bottom and sides of a brick, and with the DPC held against the back of the outer leaf, carefully slide the brick into position at the bottom of the cavity. Brick up to the top of the opening, making sure that the DPC remains in place, then repeat on the other side.

Installing Sliding Patio Doors

A wall of glass changes the appearance and outlook of a room dramatically, and by using sliding patio doors in an opening in an exterior wall *(pages 104–105)*, you can bring an additional dimension to the space in your home.

Two or more patio doors, made of toughened or laminated glass and framed in lightweight aluminium, timber or plastic, can be easily mounted on channels made from the same materials. When in use, one of the doors remains fixed in place, while the others slide past it to open. The doors are often double glazed to reduce heat loss, and some of the more expensive models can tilt in their frames to provide ventilation.

The doors and frame are mounted in a timber subframe, which lines the opening in the wall, over a damp-proof membrane. Some manufacturers supply a rebated subframe, channels, doors, and attachments such as handles, locks and stops, made to fit your opening exactly. If the subframe is not included, you will need to cut and assemble one from 100 by 50 mm hardwood for the head and jambs, plus a piece of hardwood sill. Check the minimum thicknesses of the subframe needed for the doors you are installing.

Because the details of different patio door kits vary considerably depending on the manufacturers, check the instructions carefully before starting work.

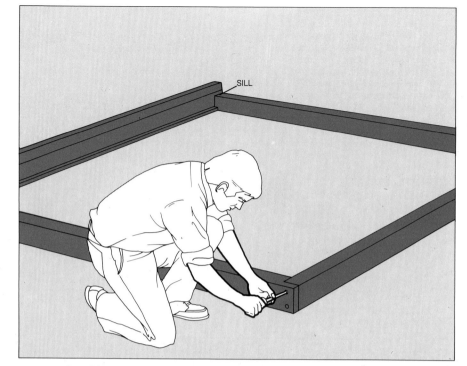

SILL

1 Preparing the subframe. Assemble the sections of the subframe on a flat surface, and screw the corners together, using countersunk screws. Then drill holes in the jambs for 75 or 87 mm No. 10 brass or galvanized countersunk screws, making sure that the holes in the subframe do not correspond to those in the aluminium frame which will be screwed into it. Insert the frame into the opening in the wall, positioning it according to the manufacturer's instructions, and mark the positions of the holes on the brickwork using a masonry drill. Remove the frame and lay it carefully aside, then drill holes in the brickwork and insert plugs.

2 Installing a damp-proof membrane. Bed a strip of damp-proof membrane on a 10 mm layer of mortar along the bottom of the opening, laying it so that it overlaps the edge of the brickwork on the outside. Spread another 10 mm layer of mortar on top of the DPC, ready to take the sill. If your opening is in a cavity wall, seal and damp-proof the cavity as on pages 104–105.

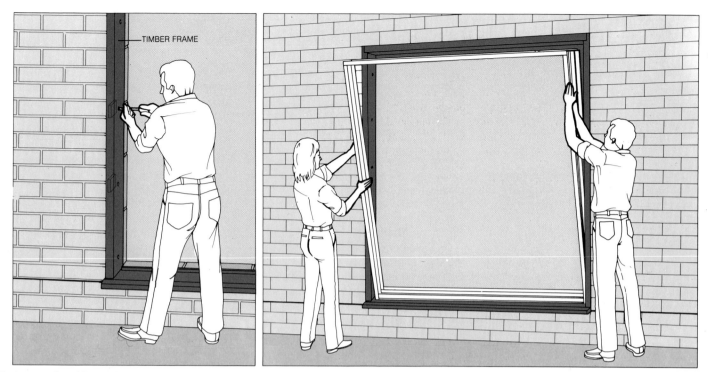

3 **Securing the subframe.** Carefully lift the subframe into the opening over the bed of mortar, packing it if necessary so that the frame is square and plumb, and the jambs are straight. Push pieces of timber as packing behind each fixing point, and screw the frame in place, countersinking the screws in the pre-drilled holes. Make good the wall, and plaster any gaps in the interior plaster at this stage, to avoid splashes of plaster damaging the aluminium frame.

4 **Installing the aluminium frame.** Place the frame sections on a flat surface, making sure that the aluminium is protected against scratches; screw the corners together. Using a mastic gun, apply sealant all round the timber subframe, along the sill, and to the underside and external joints of the aluminium frame. With a helper, lift the frame on to the timber subframe, bedding it into the mastic. Check that the frame is plumb and square, and fix it with screws to the timber subframe, making holes with an electric drill if the frame is not pre-drilled.

5 **Fitting the doors in the tracks.** Lift the fixed panel into the top channel, lower it into the bottom channel, and slide it against the jamb; fix it securely in place following the manufacturer's instructions. Fit the head closer, which prevents the fixed door from moving, then install the second door in the other track. Fit the head and sill stops for the sliding panel, then check that the rollers slide properly, adjusting at the top of the door if necessary. Complete the installation by applying a bead of non-setting mastic sealant round the frame, between the brickwork and the timber, on the inside and outside of the house.

A Labour-Saving Method for Building a Deck

In pleasant weather a wooden deck makes a versatile, sunlit space for a whole family to use. At a fraction of the cost and labour of adding a walled and roofed extension to your house, it provides an outdoor dining room, a play area for children and an entertainment centre for adults.

Because a deck represents an extension of an existing structure, it must meet the provisions of your local building code and may need a building permit. Check with your local authority before starting work.

The low-level deck, about 5 by 3 metres, shown here, is a design that can be assembled and fastened in place by two amateurs. To increase the deck area, additional decks measuring up to 5 by 3 metres can be bolted to this one. The ground beneath the deck must be clear not only of existing structures but also of all plant growth. The ground is then covered with 6-mil polythene plastic sheeting, gravel, or blind-

ing—a weak mix of 10 parts ballast to one part cement, spread dry 50 to 80 mm thick on the ground then sprinkled with water.

The low-level deck must be bolted to the wall either above or below a physical damp-proof course to avoid bridging it. Where you are planning to build a deck against a wall with a door, as in the example shown below, the door sill, and adjacent damp-proof course, must be at least 200 mm above the ground to ensure adequate ventilation beneath the frame.

On the outer edge of cleared ground you must dig holes for posts. Concrete footings for the posts must rest upon undisturbed earth below the frost line, so that freezes and thaws do not warp or crack the wood. Depending on your location, the holes you dig may be as shallow as 30 mm or as deep as 1200 mm.

In choosing the timber and fixings, your main concerns are strength and durability.

Ask your timber supplier to recommend a straight-grained, hard-wearing wood, with high resistance to decay and warping (for instance, Douglas fir, redwood, hemlock and larch). Buy wood treated with a commercial pressure process in which preservatives are forced deep into the fibres of the wood, or coat the wood yourself with one of the standard preservatives commercially available. For additional protection against rising damp, insert squares of damp-proof membrane between the concrete block piers and the wooden posts of the deck. In areas where termites are a problem, replace this damp-proof membrane by termite shield paper—a tar paper coated with copper.

Join the frame with galvanized or sherardized nails: use round-wire nails for the strutting, but for the joists annular nails will give better holding. Use metal expanding bolts to attach the frame to the wall.

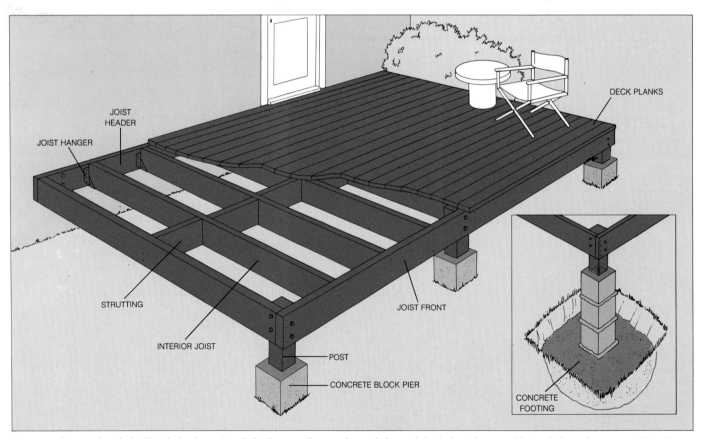

Anatomy of a wooden deck. The deck above is bolted to the side of a house. At its outer edge it is supported by posts on solid footings—300 mm slabs of concrete, topped by concrete block piers. Each pier is filled with concrete and fitted with a bolt; the posts fit on to the rag bolts, and the deck frame is bolted to the posts. Within the frame, joists are nailed directly to a joist front and are fastened to a joist header by a series of joist hangers. A staggered line of strutting gives the frame additional lateral support. The frame supports the finished floor—which consists of deck planks spaced 6 mm apart for drainage; the planks also extend 25 mm beyond the edges of the frame for decorative effect.

Building the Frame

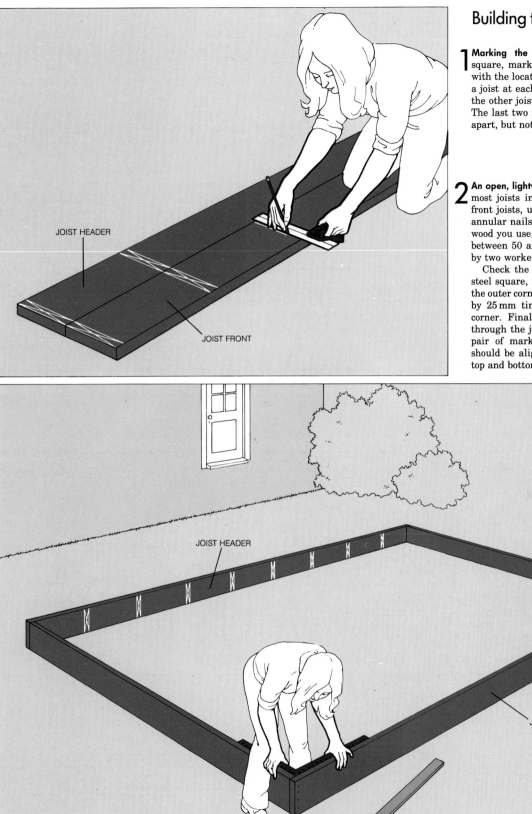

1 **Marking the boards.** Using a combination square, mark the joist header and joist front with the locations of the joists, beginning with a joist at each end of the boards, and spacing the other joists 400 mm from centre to centre. The last two marks may be less than 400 mm apart, but not more.

2 **An open, lightweight frame.** Nail the two outermost joists in place between the header and front joists, using four 125 mm round-wire or annular nails at each joint. Depending on the wood you use, the four-sided frame will weigh between 50 and 60 kilograms—easily liftable by two workers.

Check the structure for squareness with a steel square, then install temporary braces at the outer corners, using 1.2 metre lengths of 50 by 25 mm timber, nailed diagonally at each corner. Finally, drill two 12 mm bolt holes through the joist header between every other pair of marks for interior joists; the holes should be aligned vertically, 37 mm from the top and bottom of the header.

JOIST HEADER

JOIST FRONT

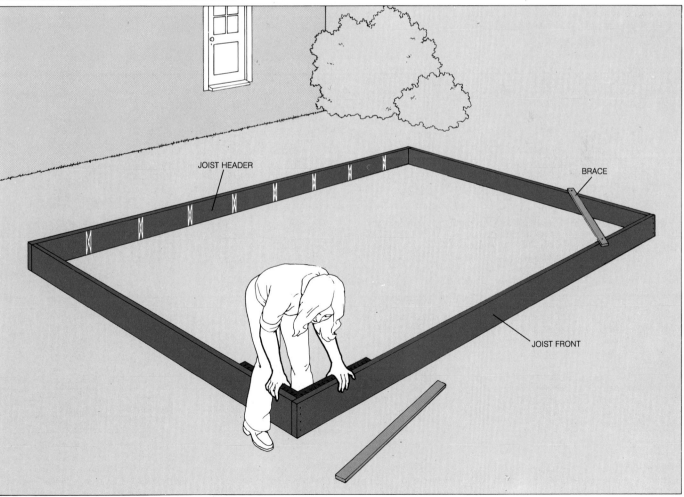

JOIST HEADER

BRACE

JOIST FRONT

Installing the Frame

1 Marking the wall. Measure the thickness of one of the deck planks and mark the wall this much below the door. Place a long straightedge on the mark, and with a helper holding the straightedge, draw a chalk line along the wall the width of the deck *(right)*, balancing a spirit level on the straightedge to ensure that it is level.

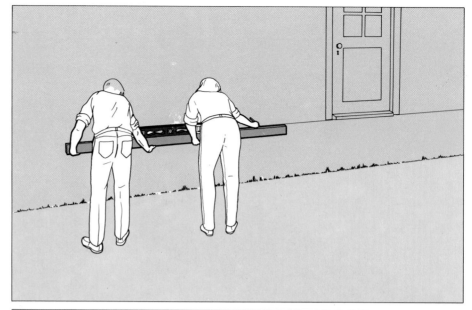

2 Positioning the frame. Drive several masonry nails into the wall at 1 metre intervals exactly the same distance down from the chalk line as the height of the frame. Then, using the nails, building blocks and wood scraps as temporary supports, set the frame into position against the house wall. Check that it is level. Using the bolt holes you have drilled in the frame as a guide, mark bolt hole positions on the wall.

3 Locating the post positions. Drive in two nails 100 mm from each outer corner of the deck frame—one nail on an end joist, the other on the joist front. Extend a string diagonally between each pair of nails, drop a plumb bob from the centre of the string and drive a stake at each point where the plumb bob meets the ground.

To locate a third post hole near the centre of the joist front—at the angle between it and the centre joist—use the mark for the centre joist as a guide. Fifty millimetres to the left or right of this mark, nail a piece of scrap wood to the joist front, with exactly 50 mm of the scrap projecting into the frame *(right)*; be sure that the scrap makes an exact right angle with the joist front. Drop a plumb bob from the projecting edge of the piece of wood and drive in a stake at the point where the bob meets the ground.

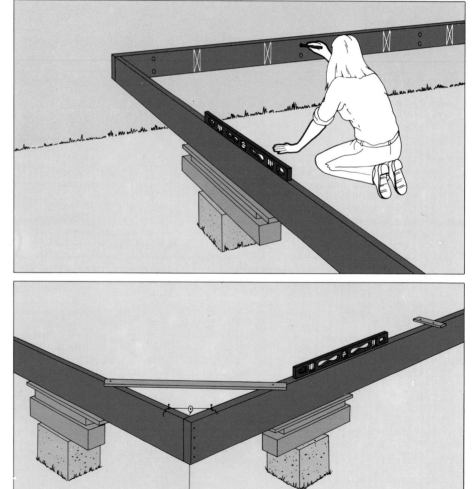

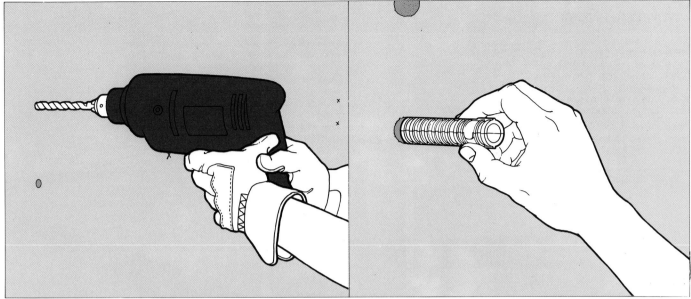

4 **Drilling the bolt holes.** With a helper, lift the frame from its temporary supports and carry it clear of the deck site. Drill 12 mm holes at the points you have marked on the wall, using an electric hammer drill fitted with a masonry bit *(above, left)*. Insert the shield of an expanding bolt in each hole *(above)*.

5 **Pouring the footings.** Using the driven stakes as guides, dig post holes, roughly 400 mm square, to the depth required—from a minimum of 300 mm to a maximum of 1200 mm. In a wheelbarrow, prepare batches of pre-mixed concrete to fill the holes with footings to the depth required. Pour the footings. Let the concrete cure for 24 to 48 hours before proceeding.

6 **Bolting the frame to the house wall.** Replace the deck frame on its temporary supports, using a spirit level to check its alignment. Then fasten the joist header of the frame to the wall of the house with the 12 mm expanding bolts, each at least 100 mm long; set washers between the bolt heads and the joist.

7 **Building a concrete block pier.** Drop plumb lines over the centres of the post holes *(page 110, Step 3)*. In each hole, using the plumb line as a centre, trowel a 200 by 200 mm bed of mortar 37 mm thick on the concrete footing, and lay a hollow-core, corner concrete block on the mortar. Trowel a second 37 mm mortar bed on the rim of the block, and continue to lay blocks until the block pier rises at least 200 mm above ground. As you work, check the vertical and horizontal alignment of the pier with a level. The following day, fill the post hole with soil to ground level.

8 **Setting post anchors.** Fill the concrete block cures with concrete and drop a plumb bob to the centre of each pier. After an hour or two, when the concrete has begun to set, insert a 150 mm rag bolt below the plumb bob, leaving 37 mm of bolt projecting above the concrete. Let the concrete cure for 24 to 48 hours, then cover the top of each pier with a square of damp-proof membrane to prevent the wooden post on top of the pier from absorbing moisture from the concrete.

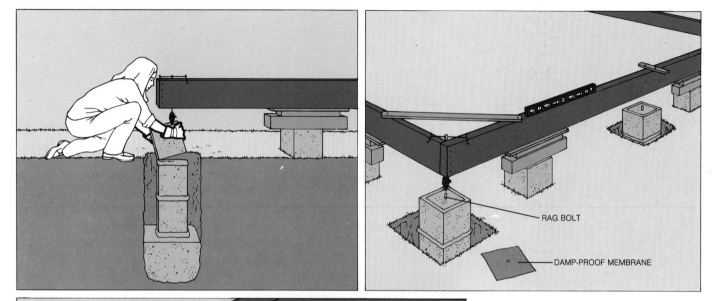

RAG BOLT

DAMP-PROOF MEMBRANE

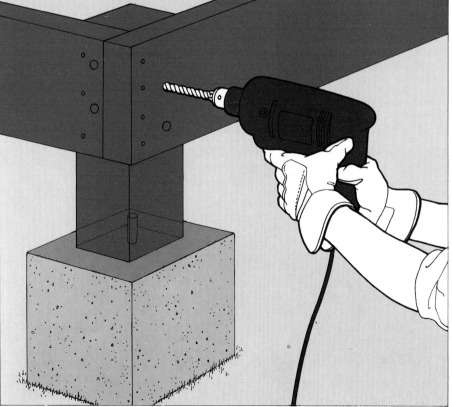

9 **Installing the posts.** Remove the plumb bobs. Cut 100 by 100 mm posts to fit between the top of each pier and the top of the deck frame. Drill a 12 mm hole 37 mm into the bottom of each post and slip the post on to a rag bolt. Nail the post into place with two or three light nails, then drill 9 mm bolt holes through the frame and into the post. Allow two holes, one above another, for the centre post, and four holes, front and side, for each of the corner posts; stagger the holes at the corners so that they do not meet. Secure the posts with 12 mm coach screws and washers.

Adding Joists and Deck Boards

STRUTTING

1 **A pattern of joists and headers.** Remove the two diagonal frame braces and cover the ground beneath the frame with gravel, blinding or 6-mil polythene sheeting weighted at the edges with bricks or stones and pierced at intervals for drainage. At each of the joist positions marked on the joist header, install a joist hanger (inset), using 37 mm annular or galvanized square twisted nails. Install the joists between the header and the joist front, nailing them into the hangers at the header end and driving four 125 mm round-wire nails through the front and into each joist at the outer end of the frame.

To complete the interior of the frame, install short headers called strutting between the joists. Set the headers alternately on and just off centre, and secure them with four 100 mm round-wire nails at each end.

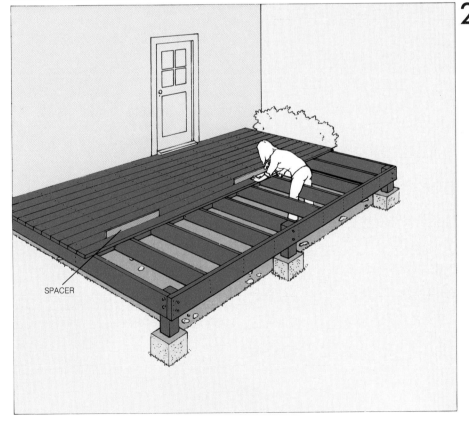

SPACER

2 **A pattern of planks.** Cover the deck frame with 100 by 37 mm planks laid across the joists and fastened at every joist with two 75 mm oval nails. Allow at least 6 mm of space between the edges and ends of the planks for drainage; to keep the spacing uniform, use 6 mm pieces of plywood set on edge as spacers between decking.

Run the decking flush to the house wall, but let it project 25 mm over the front and sides. Use a professional carpenter's trick to get a straight edge at the sides: lay the decking with an uneven edge 25 mm or more beyond the side of the frame, snap a chalk line over the planks exactly 25 mm beyond the frame, then saw through all the plank ends along the line.

Finally, seal the join between the joist header and the wall of the house with mastic.

An Overhead Covering for Deck or Patio

Adding an overhead covering to a patio or deck serves two purposes: it increases the usefulness of the outdoor living space by shielding it from the elements, and it helps to integrate the deck or patio with the architecture of the house. The overhead covering can be a leafy bower, a shady bamboo or net covering, or a permanent structure of wooden louvres.

For a deck or patio that receives sun during only part of the day, a covering that offers partial shade is generally sufficient. The trellis shown on page 117, above, supplies some shade, especially mid-morning and mid-afternoon. It can also be used as a support for climbing plants such as roses. Bamboo blinds or netting can be used as simple and inexpensive coverings for dappled shade. Their life expectancy is short but they are easy and cheap to replace.

More effective than any of these in regulating the amount of sun that reaches the deck or patio are louvres. Mounted on a north-south axis, they can be slanted to the east, to admit sunlight in the morning and block the afternoon rays. Slanting the louvres to the west reverses the effect. Placing the louvres on an east-west axis, slanting them away from the midday sun will deflect the sun at its hottest but admit some morning and evening sunlight. The angle at which you set the louvres will depend on the orientation of the deck, and the latitude at which you live. In most areas, an angle of 40 to 50 degrees will give sufficient protection, but a lower angle, about 30 degrees, will give a greater degree of shade in hotter climates.

For protection against severer weather, the trellis grid can be adapted as a frame for corrugated PVC sheeting, by fixing the beams 150 mm lower than the ledger so that the rafters are pitched slightly to allow water to run off.

As for any construction project, plan your cover with care. Use treated timber to resist decay, in sizes suited to the spans and to the weight of the covering material.

Your local authority can usually advise you on safe spans for the timber sizes you propose to use. Generally 100 by 100 mm timber is acceptable for posts. The distance a beam can span is determined by its width: a 150 by 50 mm beam is typically supported by posts spaced no more than 1.8 metres apart, a 200 by 50 mm beam by posts no more than 2.4 metres apart. In the same way, 150 by 50 mm rafters, spaced 600 mm centre to centre, span distances of up to 3 metres; 200 by 50s are often needed for 3.6 metre spans, and 250 by 50s for spans of up to 4.8 metres. The framework shown here is designed to be attached to a wooden-floored deck as shown on pages 108–113, but you can adapt it for use on a concrete patio by anchoring the posts to the slab, or by setting the posts on concrete footings *(page 108)*.

Before starting the actual construction, you may want to cut decorative ends on beams and rafters. These provide a professional touch to the finished structure.

Putting Up the Structural Support

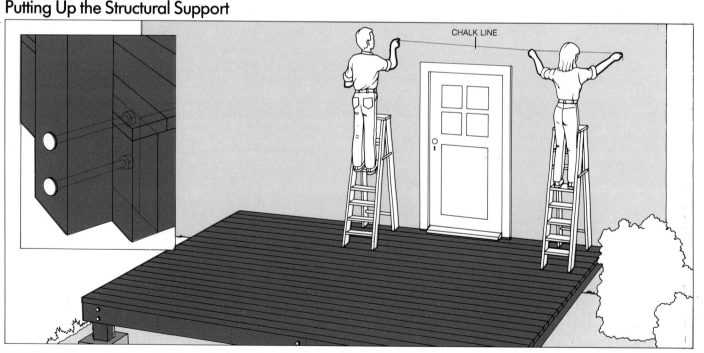

CHALK LINE

1 **Positioning a ledger on the house.** Decide on the height of the ledger, the wooden board that will hold rafters to the house, and mark this position on the wall above each corner of the doorway. Using these marks as reference points, snap a level chalk line between them. With a helper, rest the lower edge of a 150 by 37 mm ledger, the same length as the deck frame, on this line, and nail the ledger in place temporarily in order to mark holes for coach bolts or 75 mm No. 12 screws, at 300 mm intervals. Then drill holes for the bolts or screws you will be using and permanently attach the ledger to the wall.

Cut two 100 by 100 mm posts long enough to reach from a point level with the bottom of the ledger to the bottom of the front of the deck frame. Position the posts along the outer edge of the deck to align with a point 100 mm in from each end of the ledger. Secure the posts to the front of the deck frame with 150 mm-long 12 mm coach bolts *(inset)*.

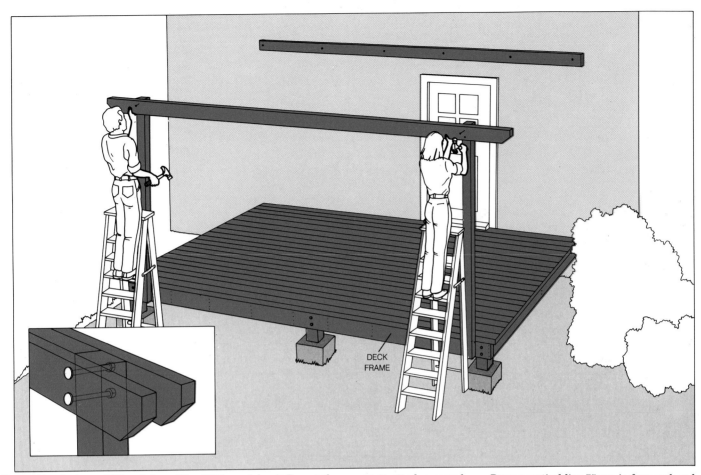

2 **Attaching the beam.** With a helper, lift a 200 by 50 mm beam 200 mm longer than the deck, and hold it against the outside of the posts, positioning it so that it extends 200 mm beyond the posts, with its upper edge flush with the tops of the posts. Check the beam with a spirit level to make sure that it is level, then secure it temporarily to each post with a 75 mm round-wire nail

(above). Repeat the process to attach a second 200 by 50 mm beam to the inner side of the posts. Using a 12 mm bit, drill two holes through each post-and-beam assembly, and secure the assembly with 12 mm coach bolts and washers *(inset).* Finally, cut seven 100 by 100 mm spacers, each 200 mm long, and nail them between the two beams at 300 mm intervals.

Draw a vertical line 75 mm in from each end of the ledger. Then subdivide the distance between these two lines into equal spaces no more than 400 mm apart. Centre and nail a 150 mm metal joist hanger over each line. Mark identically spaced lines on top of the beams, placing the first pair of vertical lines 175 mm in from the ends of the beams.

3 **Placing the rafters.** Cut 150 by 50 mm rafters, the width of the deck, plus about 200 mm for overhang, and rest the outer end of each one on top of one of the lines marked on the beams. Fit the inner end into a joist hanger, and nail it in place. At the beam end of the rafter, toenail the rafter into both sides of the beam, using two 75 mm round-wire nails on each side. Continue until all the rafters are in place.

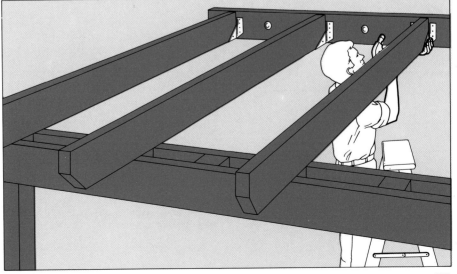

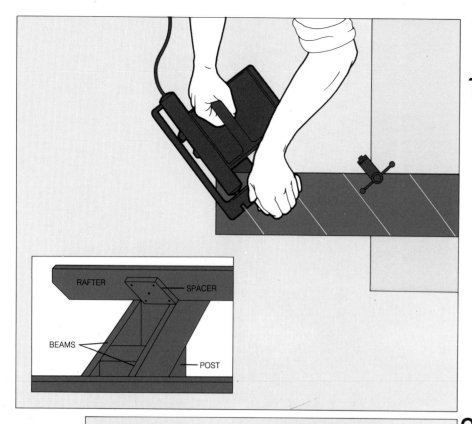

RAFTER — SPACER

BEAMS

POST

Constructing a Screen of Slanted Louvres

1 **Cutting the spacers.** With a protractor and a sliding bevel, mark a length of 100 by 25 mm timber with a series of parallel lines angled at 50 degrees, spacing the lines 100 mm apart. Then cut along the lines with a circular saw. For a structure of 3 by 2.5 metres, you will need approximately 100 pairs of spacers, requiring about 20 metres of timber.

Nail the first pair of spacers to the beam ends of two facing rafters. In the example shown, it is assumed that the deck is on the east side of the house and the goal is to admit morning sun but provide afternoon shade. For this result, set the bottom edges of the spacers flush with the bottom edges of the rafters, and set the spacers so that their downwards slant runs towards the house. The inner edges of the spacers should meet the rafter bottoms at the point where the rafters cross the inner face of the beam *(inset)*.

2 **Installing the louvres.** Cut a 150 by 25 mm louvre that will fit between the two rafters, and lay it against the first pair of spacers; nail the louvre to the edges of the spacers. Then nail a second pair of spacers to the rafters, and attach a second louvre. Continue adding spacers and louvres until the entire row has been filled. When the last louvre has been nailed into place, measure the distances from the bottom and the top of this louvre to the ledger; then, using these measurements to determine the shape needed, cut a pair of filler-spacers. Nail the filler-spacers into place. Repeat this assembly process of spacers and louvres between each pair of rafters *(inset)*.

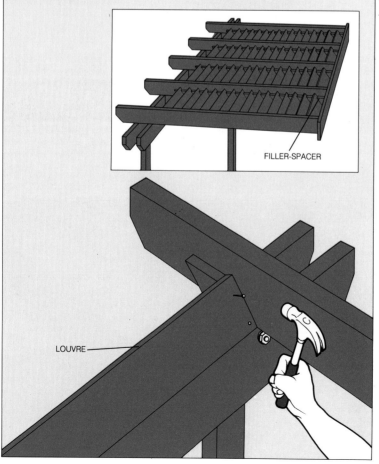

FILLER-SPACER

LOUVRE

A Covering for Varying Degrees of Shade

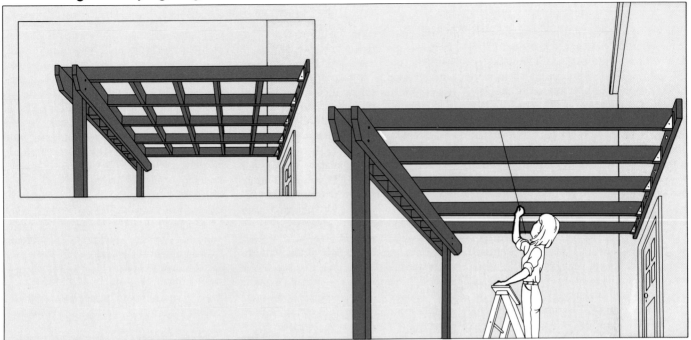

An airy trellis. Mark the bottoms of the two outer rafters at the same spacing as the joist intervals. Snap a chalk line between the pairs of marks, to transfer the measurements to intervening rafters *(above)*. Using a steel square, transfer these marks to the vertical faces of each rafter. Cut 150 by 50 mm crosspieces to fit between the rafters at the marks, and across the spacers between the beams. Nail each crosspiece to its rafters; butt-nail one end and toenail the other *(page 39)*, using 75 mm galvanized lost-head nails. Punch in the nails below the surface of the timber.

Making Panels of Net or Woven Reed

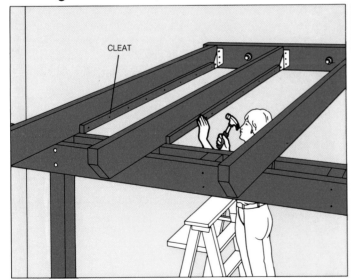

1 Installing support cleats. To support panels of woven-reed fencing or netting, nail 50 by 25 mm cleats along both the lower edges of each rafter. Make the cleats long enough to extend from the inner face of the inner beam to the joist hanger.

Make up a frame to fit between each pair of rafters, using four pieces of 50 by 50 mm timber. Glue and nail the shorter end pieces across the ends of the longer side pieces.

2 Attaching reeds. Lay woven-reed fencing or netting, available at garden centres, across the wooden frame as shown above, fastening it to the frame on all edges with heavy duty staples spaced 50 to 75 mm apart. Trim off excess fencing. Repeat for each frame. Lower the frames into place, allowing them to rest loosely on top of the cleats *(inset)*.

Expanding a House by Converting a Garage

Converting a garage into potential new living space involves replacing the car-entry door with a permanent wall and finishing the new wall's exterior to match or contrast with the finish of the rest of the garage and the house.

An old-fashioned garage door that opens outwards needs only to be taken off its hinges. You may prefer to entrust to a contractor the more complex task of removing a heavy, spring-powered sectional door, but as the drawings illustrate, it is possible to do it yourself.

Framing out the opening demands only the simple carpentry described on pages 36–39. If the converted garage is to be permanently occupied, you will need to apply for planning permission. For occasional use, residential building codes usually require that a converted garage should admit natural light through a window, that it has door space roughly equal to one-tenth of its floor area, and that at least half of this area must provide a ventilation opening. The easiest place to install a door or a factory-made window unit is in the new wall.

Finish the outside of the wall first; line it with breather paper, which is resistant to moisture, and cover it with weatherproof cladding. Working from the inside, pack the frame with glass fibre insulation material. To finish the interior wall, line the frame with a vapour barrier, and then cover it with sheets of foil-backed plasterboard nailed to wooden battens.

To complete the exterior of the wall underneath the window, it is simplest not to attempt a match with the existing exterior of the house. Masonry, especially, presents a number of difficulties: rendering calls for professional skills, and new bricks, even if identical to the original house bricks, will look different until they have weathered for many years. Instead, select a contrasting material, such as metal, plastic or wooden shiplap cladding which gives a good weatherproof finish.

Wooden cladding is nailed directly into the studs, and is sealed with lead flashing under the window. Aluminium or plastic cladding is installed over a metal frame which is supplied by the manufacturer, and is fixed to the studs.

To conceal the fact that your new room was once a garage, you may need to break up and remove the drive apron. If you merely wish to mask the effect of a drive halting abruptly at the base of a wall, you can level the apron with concrete and build a plant container across the new surface.

Removing a Sectional Door

1 **Loosening the spring-locking bolts.** If the weight of your sectional garage door is countered by a wind-up spring over the opening, lower the door to get at the spring. Take great care in unwinding the spring, which is at maximum tension with the door down. For this purpose use two strong metal winding bars—both at least 450 mm long and made of cold-rolled steel. The manufacturers may have provided them when the door was installed. Insert one bar in one of the holes in the winding cone. It should fit snugly. Keeping a firm grip on the rod to restrain the cone, loosen the cone's spring-locking bolts.

2 **Unwinding the spring.** Slowly release the spring, alternating the bars in the cone holes as the cone turns. Grip the bars near their ends to exert the fullest possible leverage on the spring. When the spring has unwound and the wire cable connecting it to the door is slack, unfasten the cable from the cable bracket.

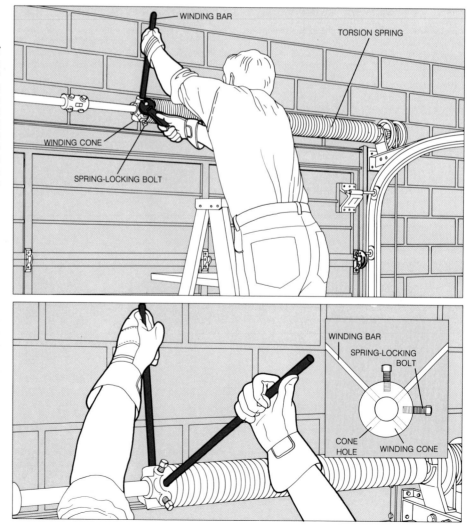

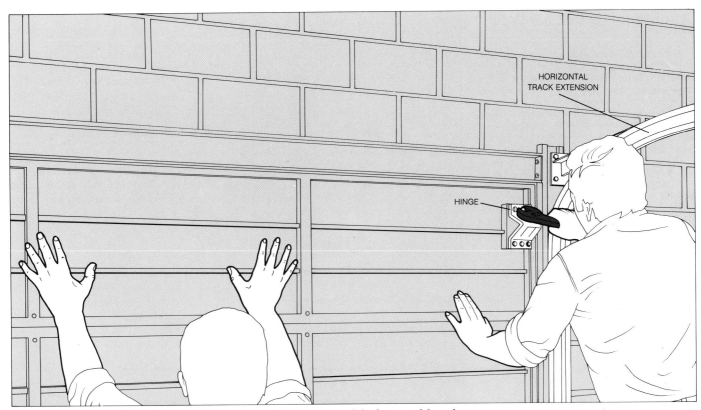

HORIZONTAL TRACK EXTENSION

HINGE

3 **Dismantling the door.** Dismantle any sectional garage door from the top down. Remove the hinges and fixtures from the top section, then the section itself. Similarly remove each succeeding section. Remove a torsion shaft by unbolting it from the top member of the frame, and from the tops of the horizontal track extensions. Begin track removal at the rear of the garage. Unbolt the horizontal tracks from their supports, then unscrew the frame from the opening.

Removing a Side-Spring Door

Unhooking vertical extension springs. If the door has a vertical extension spring on each side, raise the door to the open horizontal position to decrease spring tension. Prop the door open with two 100 by 50 mm pieces of timber. Carefully disengage one spring from its bottom anchor hook or adjuster, and unclip its top from the grooved pin. Remove the other spring in the same way. Take down the props and lower the door. Wedge it in position and unscrew the bottom and wheel brackets. Remove the door, unscrew the lever and track brackets, and take out the lever arms and tracks.

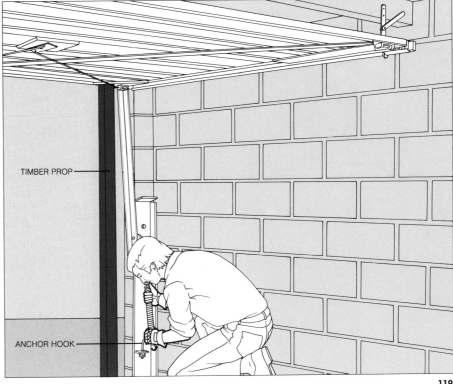

TIMBER PROP

ANCHOR HOOK

A Frame for an Exterior Wall

A weatherproof timber wall. A ready-made window unit set into a simple timber stud frame *(pages 36–39)* replaces the door in a converted garage. A damp-proof course is laid under the sole plate on the concrete slab of the garage floor. The outside of the wall is lined with breather paper, which allows moisture to escape from the room while preventing it from coming in, and is finished with weatherproof shiplap cladding.

Glass fibre insulating material fills the frame which is then lined on the inside with a vapour barrier. The frame and the garage wall are finished inside with foil-backed plasterboard.

The new wall is completed by installing the window unit, and is sealed using lead flashing dressed over the exterior cladding.

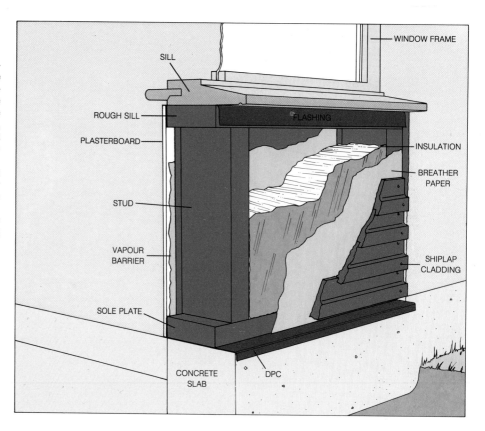

Starting the Wall

1 **Preparing the opening.** Remove the timber door-frame using a hammer and chisel, or by unscrewing it from the wall. Lay a strip of damp-proof membrane on a 10 mm bed of mortar along the edge of the opening, as shown on page 106.

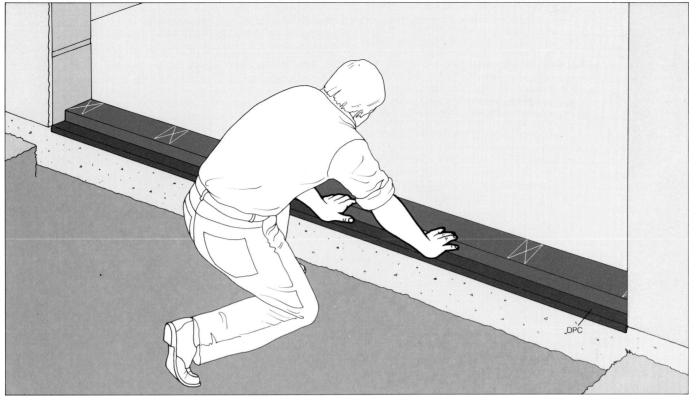

2 **Positioning the sole plate.** To make a sole plate and rough sill, cut two pieces of 100 by 50 mm timber, treated with wood preservative, to fit the opening. At either end of one piece, mark off a 50 mm-wide area for studs; then continue to mark off 50 mm areas at 400 mm intervals between these marks. Transfer the markings to the other timber *(page 36, Step 1)*. Bed the sole plate on top of the damp-proof membrane in a 10 mm layer of mortar. The sole plate should be flush with the interior edge of the wall and set back from the outer edge.

3 **Building the wall frame.** Measure the height of the window unit. Take the measurement to the opening and, working from the top, mark the wall on both sides. Measure from this mark to the sole plate and subtract 50 mm for the rough sill. Cut the required number of studs to this length from 100 by 50 mm treated timber. Nail the studs in the marked positions on the rough sill. Lift the frame over the sole plate, and toenail the bottom of the studs in place *(page 39)*.

Lining and Finishing
the Frame

1 **Waterproofing the exterior.** Mark the positions of the stud centres on the outside edge of the opening. Working on the outside, staple moistureproof breather paper to the stud wall at 150 mm intervals along the edges of the frame, and at 300 mm intervals along the studs, using the marks as guidelines. Where it is necessary to make joins, site them over studs.

2 **Fitting shiplap cladding.** Starting at the top of the wall frame under the window sill, nail shiplap boards into the studs with sherardized lost-head nails, ensuring that each nail pierces only one piece of board. Cut the last board, if necessary, to fit over the concrete slab.

3 **Lining the inside of the wall.** Fill the stud frame from the inside with glass fibre insulating material. Staple polythene vapour barrier to the frame over the glass fibre. Fix 50 by 37 mm vertical battens to the whole of the inside wall at 400 mm intervals, using 63 mm cut nails or 75 mm No. 8 screws; also fix battens to the studs using 63 mm lost-head nails. Cover the whole of the interior wall and frame with foil-backed plasterboard, as shown on pages 44—47.

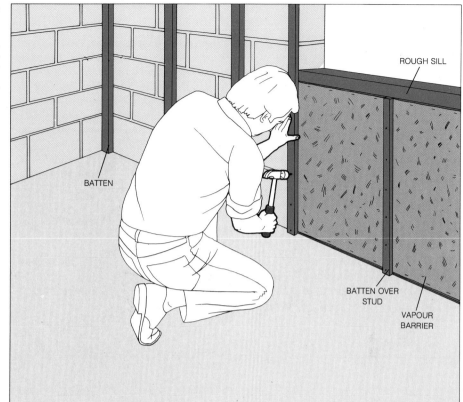

ROUGH SILL

BATTEN

BATTEN OVER
STUD

VAPOUR
BARRIER

4 **Installing the window.** Fit lead flashing over the rough sill, flush with the inner surface of the wall, and overlapping the outer edge by 100 mm. With a helper, lift the window frame into the opening *(above)*, positioning it so that the drip groove on the sill hangs clear of the cladding. Fix the frame into the mortar joints of the walls, using 75 or 100 mm No. 10 screws or 100 mm cut nails, before glazing the window.

Dress the flashing over the cladding, then seal the gap between the edges of the cladding and the wall with mastic filler.

Picture Credits

The sources for the illustrations in this book are shown below. Credits for the illustrations from left to right are separated by semicolons, from top to bottom by dashes.

Cover: Martin Brigdale. 6: Martin Brigdale. 8: Drawings by Vicki Vebell. 9: Drawings by Oxford Illustrators Ltd. 10–17: Drawings by Ray Skibinski. 18: Stephen R. Brown. 20–25: Drawings by John Massey. 26–32: Drawings by Walter Hilmers Jr. 33: Drawings by Oxford Illustrators Ltd. 34: John Neubauer. 36–38: Drawings by Whitman Studio Inc. 39: Drawing by Whitman Studio Inc.—Drawing by Oxford Illustrators Ltd; Drawing by Whitman Studio Inc. 40, 41: Drawings by Whitman Studio Inc. 42: Drawings by Peter McGinn. 43: Drawing by Peter McGinn—Drawing by Oxford Illustrators Ltd. 44: Drawings by Peter McGinn—Drawing by Oxford Illustrators Ltd. 45: Drawings by Peter McGinn. 46: Drawing by Oxford Illustrators Ltd.—Drawings by Forte Inc. 47: Drawings by Forte Inc. 48, 49: Drawings by Oxford Illustrators Ltd. 50: Drawing by Whitman Studio Inc. 51: Drawing by Oxford Illustrators Ltd.—Drawings by Whitman Studio Inc.; Drawing by Oxford Illustrators Ltd. 52: Drawings by Forte Inc. 53: Drawing by John Massey; Drawings by Nick Fasciano. 54, 55: Drawings by Forte Inc. 56: Drawing by Oxford Illustrators Ltd. 57, 58: Drawings by Nick Fasciano. 59–63: Drawings by Oxford Illustrators Ltd. 64: Martin Brigdale. 66: Drawing by Peter McGinn; Drawing by Hayward and Martin Ltd. 67: Drawing by Hayward and Martin Ltd.—Drawings by Peter McGinn. 68, 69: Drawings by Peter McGinn. 70, 71: Drawings by Adolph E. Brotman. 72, 73: Drawings by Peter McGinn. 74: Drawing by Adolph E. Brotman—Drawing by Vicki Vebell. 75: Drawings by Vicki Vebell. 76: Drawings by Hayward and Martin Ltd. 77: Drawing by Adolph E. Brotman—Drawing by Hayward and Martin Ltd. 78: Drawings by Adolph E. Brotman. 79: Drawings by Vicki Vebell. 80: Drawings by Adolph E. Brotman. 81: Drawing by Adolph E. Brotman—Drawings by Hayward and Martin Ltd. 82: Martin Brigdale. 84–97: Drawings by Oxford Illustrators Ltd. 98: Drawings by Tom Gladden. 99: Drawings by Tom Gladden; Drawing by Oxford Illustrators Ltd. 100: Martin Brigdale. 102–107: Drawings by Oxford Illustrators Ltd. 108, 109: Drawings by Peter McGinn. 110: Drawing by Oxford Illustrators Ltd—Drawings by Peter McGinn. 111–113: Drawings by Peter McGinn. 114–117: Drawings by James Anderson. 118: Drawings by John Sagan. 119: Drawings by Oxford Illustrators Ltd. 120: Drawing by Oxford Illustrators Ltd.—Drawing by John Sagan. 121: Drawings by John Sagan. 122: Drawing by John Sagan—Drawing by Oxford Illustrators Ltd. 123: Drawings by Oxford Illustrators Ltd.

Acknowledgements

The editors would like to extend special thanks to Veronique Despreaux, Dip. Arch., Martin Leighton, Caroline Manyon, and Richard Pilling, London; and Tim Fraser, Sydney. They also wish to thank the following: Brown and Tawse Ltd., London; John Carr Joinery Sales Ltd.; Catnic Ltd., Caerphilly, Mid Glamorgan; The Concrete Lintels Association; Dawson and Co. Builders' Merchants Ltd., London; Groupe Maison Familiale, Cambrai; Paul Hakius, Stuttgart; Hörmann (UK) Ltd., Whetstone, Leics.; W. König, Dipl. Ing., Bad Salzuflen; Maisons Phénix, Paris; Marley Buildings Ltd., Guildford, Surrey; The W.H. Newson Group of Companies; Priday's, London; Producta Ltd.; Vicki Robinson, London; The Velux Company Ltd. and Mr D. Denholm.

Index/Glossary

Metric Conversion Chart

Approximate equivalents—length

Millimetres to inches		Inches to millimetres	
1	1/32	1/32	1
2	1/16	1/16	2
3	1/8	1/8	3
4	5/32	3/16	5
5	3/16	1/4	6
6	1/4	5/16	8
7	9/32	3/8	10
8	5/16	7/16	11
9	11/32	1/2	13
10 (1cm)	3/8	9/16	14
11	7/16	5/8	16
12	15/32	11/16	17
13	1/2	3/4	19
14	9/16	13/16	21
15	19/32	7/8	22
16	5/8	15/16	24
17	11/16	1	25
18	23/32	2	51
19	3/4	3	76
20	25/32	4	102
25	1	5	127
30	1 3/16	6	152
40	1 9/16	7	178
50	1 15/16	8	203
60	2 3/8	9	229
70	2 3/4	10	254
80	3 1/8	11	279
90	3 9/16	12 (1ft)	305
100	3 15/16	13	330
200	7 7/8	14	356
300	11 13/16	15	381
400	15 3/4	16	406
500	19 11/16	17	432
600	23 5/8	18	457
700	27 9/16	19	483
800	31 1/2	20	508
900	35 7/16	24 (2ft)	610
1000 (1m)	39 3/8	Yards to metres	

Metres to feet/inches		1	0.914
2	6' 7"	2	1.83
3	9' 10"	3	2.74
4	13' 1"	4	3.65
5	16' 5"	5	4.57
6	19' 8"	6	5.49
7	23' 0"	7	6.40
8	26' 3"	8	7.32
9	29' 6"	9	8.23
10	32' 10"	10	9.14
20	65' 7"	20	18.29
50	164' 0"	50	45.72
100	328' 7"	100	91.44

Conversion factors

Length

1 millimetre (mm)	= 0.0394 in
1 centimetre (cm)/10 mm	= 0.3937 in
1 metre/100 cm	= 39.37 in/3.281 ft/1.094 yd
1 kilometre (km)/1000 metres	= 1093.6 yd/0.6214 mile
1 inch (in)	= 25.4 mm/2.54 cm
1 foot (ft)/12 in	= 304.8 mm/30.48 cm/0.3048 metre
1 yard (yd)/3 ft	= 914.4 mm/91.44 cm/0.9144 metre
1 mile/1760 yd	= 1609.344 metres/1.609 km

Area

1 square centimetre (sq cm)/ 100 square millimetres (sq mm)	= 0.155 sq in
1 square metre (sq metre)/10,000 sq cm	= 10.764 sq ft/1.196 sq yd
1 are/100 sq metres	= 119.60 sq yd/0.0247 acre
1 hectare (ha)/100 ares	= 2.471 acres/0.00386 sq mile
1 square inch (sq in)	= 645.16 sq mm/6.4516 sq cm
1 square foot (sq ft)/144 sq in	= 929.03 sq cm
1 square yard (sq yd)/9 sq ft	= 8361.3 sq cm/0.8361 sq metre
1 acre/4840 sq yd	= 4046.9 sq metres/0.4047 ha
1 square mile/640 acres	= 259 ha/2.59 sq km

Volume

1 cubic centimetre (cu cm)/ 1000 cubic millimetres (cu mm)	= 0.0610 cu in
1 cubic decimetre (cu dm)/1000 cu cm	= 61.024 cu in/0.0353 cu ft
1 cubic metre/1000 cu dm	= 35.3146 cu ft/1.308 cu yd
1 cu cm	= 1 millilitre (ml)
1 cu dm	= 1 litre see **Capacity**
1 cubic inch (cu in)	= 16.3871 cu cm
1 cubic foot (cu ft)/1728 cu in	= 28.3168 cu cm/0.0283 cu metre
1 cubic yard (cu yd)/27 cu ft	= 0.7646 cu metre

Capacity

1 litre	= 1.7598 pt/0.8799 qt/0.22 gal
1 pint (pt)	= 0.568 litre
1 quart (qt)	= 1.137 litres
1 gallon (gal)	= 4.546 litres

Weight

1 gram (g)	= 0.035 oz
1 kilogram (kg)/1000 g	= 2.20 lb/35.2 oz
1 tonne/1000 kg	= 2204.6 lb/0.9842 ton
1 ounce (oz)	= 28.35 g
1 pound (lb)	= 0.4536 kg
1 ton	= 1016 kg

Pressure

1 gram per square metre (g/metre^2)	= 0.0292 oz/sq yd
1 gram per square centimetre (g/cm^2)	= 0.226 oz/sq in
1 kilogram per square centimetre (kg/cm^2)	= 14.226 lb/sq in
1 kilogram per square metre (kg/metre^2)	= 0.205 lb/sq ft
1 pound per square foot (lb/ft^2)	= 4.882 kg/metre^2
1 pound per square inch (lb/in^2)	= 703.07 kg/metre^2
1 ounce per square yard (oz/yd^2)	= 33.91 g/metre^2
1 ounce per square foot (oz/ft^2)	= 305.15 g/metre^2

Temperature

To convert °F to °C, subtract 32, then divide by 9 and multiply by 5
To convert °C to °F, divide by 5 and multiply by 9, then add 32

Phototypeset by Tradespools Limited, Frome, Somerset
Printed and bound by Artes Gráficas, Toledo, SA, Spain
D. L. TO:664-1985